MW00563164

THE SOUTHERN FOODWAYS ALLIANCE GUIDE TO COCKTAILS

The Southern Foodways Alliance Guide *to* Cocktails

SARA CAMP MILAM AND JERRY SLATER

PHOTOGRAPHS BY ANDREW THOMAS LEE

Published in association with the Southern Foodways Alliance, an institute of the Center for the Study of Southern Culture at the University of Mississippi

THE UNIVERSITY OF GEORGIA PRESS   ATHENS

This publication is made possible in part through a grant
from the Bradley Hale Fund for Southern Studies.

© 2017 by the University of Georgia Press
Athens, Georgia 30602
www.ugapress.org
All rights reserved
Designed by Erin Kirk New
Set in Miller Text with Playfair display
Printed and bound by Asia Pacific Offset
The paper in this book meets the guidelines for
permanence and durability of the Committee on
Production Guidelines for Book Longevity of the
Council on Library Resources.

Most University of Georgia Press titles are
available from popular e-book vendors.

Printed in China

21 20 19 18 17 C 5 4 3 2 1

Library of Congress Cataloging-in-Publication Data
Names: Milam, Sara Camp, author. | Slater, Jerry, 1971– author. |
    Lee, Andrew Thomas, photographer.
Title: The southern foodways alliance guide to cocktails /
    Sara Camp Milam and Jerry Slater ; photographs by
    Andrew Thomas Lee.
Description: Athens : University of Georgia Press, [2017]
Identifiers: LCCN 2017009542 | ISBN 9780820351599 (hardcover :
    alk. paper)
Subjects: LCSH: Cocktails. | BISAC: COOKING / Beverages /
    Bartending. | LCGFT: Cookbooks.
Classification: LCC TX951 .M438 2017 | DDC 641.87/4—dc23
    LC record available at https://lccn.loc.gov/2017009542

Contents

Sidebars

Preface

WELCOME TO *The Southern Foodways Alliance Guide to Cocktails*. The Southern Foodways Alliance (SFA) is a documentary-focused academic institution with a sense of humor and a soft spot for the absurd. (See our 2007 bacon forest, our 2013 cake-versus-pie debate, and our 2015 shrimp-and-grits dunking booth.) We wrote and edited a book about cocktails because we believe that well-told stories complement well-mixed drinks. In the pages that follow, we serve up more than eighty drink recipes and dozens of stories.

Since 1999 the SFA has captured and shared narratives of barbecue, tamales, and gumbo. Of tacos, plate lunches, and boudin. When SFA shares stories about those foods, we honor the men and women who grow, prepare, and serve them. We apply that same approach to cocktails. What we pour in our glasses, where we do the pouring, and with whom we do the drinking: Those matters reveal truths about our values and our identity in a diverse and changing region.

This is a cocktail book. If you came looking for muscadine wine, heirloom cider, or craft IPA, look elsewhere. That's not to say that fermented (as opposed to distilled) spirits don't matter in our region. We had to draw the line somewhere, and we drew it at mixed liquor drinks, whose origins are just about as old as our country itself. From those late eighteenth-century toddies and slings evolved the cocktail, a class of drink that became popular in the first half of the nineteenth century and originally called for a spirit base cut with water, sugar, and bitters. When we say "cocktail" today, we're talking about any single-serving mixed liquor drink; the bitters are no longer a categorical requirement, though you'll find them in abundance in this volume. Old habits die hard—and taste good.

You hold in your hands an SFA-curated, bartender-developed, contemporary drink manifesto from the South. It's sometimes opinionated but—we hope!—never judgmental. My coeditor is Jerry Slater, a veteran bartender who hails from West Virginia, Indiana, and Kentucky. He put himself through college while working in restaurants, earning a degree in English literature, and got serious about a career in the food and beverage business during a stint at Charlie Trotter's in Chicago. Following seven years in Louisville, most of them at the historic Seelbach Hotel, Slater made his way to Atlanta, where he was an opening partner and developed the cocktail program at One Flew South in

Hartsfield-Jackson International Airport. From 2010 to 2016 he owned and operated H. Harper Station, a bar and restaurant in Atlanta's Reynoldstown neighborhood. More recently Slater and his wife, Krista, an artist and wine professional, have taken to country life in rural Bostwick, Georgia. Between consulting, writing, and guest bartending gigs, they have their sights set on a new venture up the road in Athens.

For this book, Slater and I gathered recipes both classic and contemporary from more than twenty bartenders. They are men and women who span the region from Washington, D.C., to Austin, Texas, and their tastes are as diverse as their backgrounds. You'll meet Alba Huerta, a native of Monterrey, Mexico, whose Houston bar, Julep, brings together the region's history and future, often in a single glass. And Paul Calvert, a literary scholar turned mixologist who brings his book learning to bear at Atlanta's Ticonderoga Club. And more than a dozen others, each with her or his own perspective on, and approach to, the region's drinkways. Take a careful look at the drink names and ingredient lists. You'll find references to Southern literature, Scottish alternative rock, native fruits, and forgotten spirits. In other words, the bartenders with whom we have partnered are not only good mixologists, they are good company. Seek them out, thank them for us, and tip them well. (You can read more about each of them at the end of the book.)

We'd never recommend drinking on an empty stomach. To steer clear of that problem, we tapped Vishwesh Bhatt, the chef at Snackbar, our favorite hometown watering hole in Oxford, Mississippi. He developed ten snacks to pair with your favorite cocktail, whatever it might be. Some are Southern classics. Others are riffs on regional flavors filtered through Bhatt's Indian American experience.

The stories, which comprise a third leg of this barstool, are there to give you something to talk about at your next cocktail party. We don't intend to make you into a walking encyclopedia of Southern cocktail history. After reading this book, and mixing a few drinks, you will know enough spirituous lore to impress friends, family, and barmates. This book is a point of departure, not a Last Word. (Though we do love that Prohibition-era gin and Chartreuse drink.) Think of this guide as a library of drink possibilities, based on proven excellence and future prospects.

Cheers, and happy reading.

SARA CAMP MILAM

THE SOUTHERN FOODWAYS ALLIANCE GUIDE TO COCKTAILS

Introduction

DRINKING IN THE SOUTH IS COMPLICATED. Literal restrictions and societal landmines discourage imbibing here. So do many denominations of the Protestant church. An equal and opposite force attracts us to share a whiskey on the porch, to toast our victories and losses in communality. Our culture and history run brown with booze like a black ribbon of coal under an Appalachian mountain. The push and pull of joyous indulgence and ruinous overindulgence define our favorite pastimes, from sports to music to dining.

Sports and alcohol in the South share a tangled history. No alcohol has been sold at a Southeastern Conference football stadium in more than thirty years. Yet fans still drink at tailgates. And more than a few sneak hip flasks into stadiums. NASCAR is soaked in illegal alcohol. Bootleggers like Junior Johnson, transporting illegal whiskey in autos modified to evade revenue agents, drove the development of stock car racing, a sport that now promotes itself as family friendly. And the Kentucky Derby, billed as "the most exciting two minutes in sports," is so soaked in Mint Juleps that it's sometimes difficult to tell where the horse racing ends and the bourbon marketing begins.

Drinking informs our music, too. Jazz, like the cocktail, is an American invention. We celebrate those who riff smartly on the classics, whether on the stage or behind the bar. Jelly Roll Morton, the jazz progenitor, began his career in the sporting houses of New Orleans, where drinks flowed and prostitution flourished.

In southern Alabama, a kid named Hiram King "Hank" Williams emerged in the 1940s as one of the nation's premier interpreters of country music. Williams sang gospel songs like "I Saw the Light" while drinking himself to death. That tension, between religion and perdition, between dry and wet, pervades this place. Modern Southern music plays a similar Janus-faced role. The Atlanta rapper Ludacris brags about "Everybody Drunk." In "Cover Me Up," Jason Isbell of Muscle Shoals, Alabama, sings of how he "swore off that stuff."

Drink pervades Southern literature, too. Carson McCullers of Columbus, Georgia, drank a mixture of hot tea and sherry she called Sonnie Boy from a thermos she kept by her typewriter. Tennessee Williams, born in Columbus, Mississippi, believed that alcohol calmed the demons on display in works like his play *The Glass Menagerie*.

In *Cat on a Hot Tin Roof* the character Brick Pollitt references "the click I get in my head when I've had enough of this stuff to make me peaceful." When Tennessee Williams was a boy, Mississippi was a tough place to get a drink. The state did not legalize liquor sales until 1966. That's not to say that it was dry. A quick perusal of the blues catalog reveals abundant tales of jake-leg whiskey.

Throughout the contemporary South, our relationship to alcohol remains conflicted. Take Kentucky. As the reputation of bourbon and pride in that native spirit continue to climb, thirty-three Kentucky counties still refuse to allow sales of the stuff. As recently as 2013, Kentucky had more dry counties than wet.

The high priest of duplicity in drinking may have been Noah "Soggy" Sweat Jr., who while serving in Mississippi state legislature in the early 1950s delivered what is now known as "the whiskey speech." Judge Sweat declared that whiskey was "the devil's brew [and] the poison scourge." He also praised liquor as the "oil of conversation," the "philosophical wine." Like many in the South, he straddled the wet-dry divide and found that position quite comfortable.

THE COCKTAILS IN THIS BOOK meet one or more of the following criteria: (1) They were conceived or popularized in the South. (2) They use Southern ingredients, like peaches from Georgia or honeysuckle vodka from Mississippi. (3) They were concocted or recommended by some of the best bartenders in the region. Alongside the call-outs for Coca-Cola, Cheerwine, and Kentucky bourbon, you'll see recipes that incorporate Italian amaros, French fortified wines, Mexican tequilas. Ours is a global South.

Just a couple of notes before getting into the drink of the matter. Although the word "mixologist" is about a century and a half old (it first appeared in print in 1856), we believe that hospitality is just as important as drink-making talent. Maybe more so. A great professional bartender makes good conversation and keeps a clean and organized workspace. This goes for the home bar, too. Organize your party so you can be present. That's what your friends will remember, not your bitters collection. Don't feel like you need to run out and buy every ingredient in the book. Build your collection of tools and spirits over time.

When using this book, you can assume a couple of things. When we say juice, we mean fresh. You will notice the difference. Feel free to backslide once in a while. It's okay if you buy a bottle of grapefruit juice to make the Ruby Slipper on page 18. Your brunch party would rather laugh with you on the porch than watch you squeeze citrus. The same goes for herbs, eggs, or cream. Buy fresh, quality ingredients. But don't stress out. Don't worry about liquor brands, either. Use what you know you like, or try something new if you're feeling adventurous. When we recommend a brand in a recipe in this book, it's for one of a couple of reasons: Either the aging process, distilling style, or provenance of the ingredient makes a difference in the flavor profile of the finished drink (this is especially the case with rum drinks), or the spirit is one of a kind (if there's an artichoke amaro liqueur that's not Cynar, you'd probably have to go to an off-the-map Italian village to find it). For the most part, we favor ingredients that are widely available at your local liquor store or online. When we deviate from that democratic approach, it's because we truly believe the drink is a just reward for the challenge of tracking down or making the special ingredients.

Finally, a note about organization. The first ten chapters of the book are structured around iconic cocktails, moving roughly in order of increasing strength. An opening essay argues for each drink's status in the regional pantheon. The recipes that follow are kindred spirits. (Forgive the pun.) That means the Brandy Milk Punch chapter includes breakfast drinks, brunch drinks, and other light or creamy fare. "Ramos Gin Fizz" includes sours and fizzes that may or may not contain eggs. In the French 75 chapter we include drinks topped with spirited bubbles, be they champagne, cider, or beer. Under "Mint Julep" you will find refreshing drinks, mostly on crushed ice, like juleps, cobblers, and frappés. By the middle of the book we defend the Hurricane and resolve to take ourselves less than seriously. The second movement continues with the Manhattan, a drink that *is* taken seriously in the South; stirred and boozy drinks, including the Martini, live here. The chapter on the Old-Fashioned is straightforward and hopefully enlightening. After that comes the Sazerac, the New Orleans classic to which so many Southern bartenders have concocted odes. We stay in New Orleans for the Vieux Carré and its variations, including those based on similar ratios, like the Negroni. We finish with punch, for festive occasions or no-reason-needed communing over the bowl.

Cheers!

JERRY SLATER

Drink Recipes

Eighty-Eight Recipes to Slake Your Thirst

1

Day Drinking
Brandy Milk Punch

Brandy, You're a Fine Girl

Quick—name a cocktail mixed with dairy. You thought of The Dude's White Russian in *The Big Lebowski*, didn't you? You're picturing Jeff Bridges wandering the supermarket aisles in his bathrobe and sunglasses, sniffing a carton of half-and-half to test its freshness before shuffling to the cashier and writing a check for sixty-nine cents.

Natives of Louisiana and Mississippi might picture another scene. For them, a dairy cocktail means milk punch, made with brandy, bourbon, or rum. It's a breakfast or brunch drink that marks festive daytime occasions, such as tailgating before a football game or celebrating a milestone birthday with lunch at Galatoire's or opening presents on a holiday morning.

We don't tend to think of brandy as a cocktail base for the twenty-first century, but along with rum, it was the South's staple spirit. Before the Mint Julep became synonymous with bourbon and the Sazerac morphed into a rye vehicle, both were brandy drinks. Elizabeth Williams of the Southern Food & Beverage Museum posits that imported brandy such as cognac, distilled from grapes, was the spirit of choice among early New Orleans tipplers because they came from the wine-drinking cultures of France and Spain. (Settlers in the Mid-Atlantic and Southeast distilled brandy from homegrown apples and peaches.) The phylloxera epidemic of the 1800s, which decimated European grapevines, and the rise of domestic distilling during the same period, meant that by the end of the nineteenth century, brandy was no longer the region's favored distilled spirit.

While some recipes suggest that you can mix a fine milk punch with bourbon, rum, or even scotch (we're a little skeptical of that last one), purists and seasoned day drinkers swear by the winey tang of brandy.

Though it's classified as a punch, this drink can be shaken one serving at a time or mixed in larger batches. According to cocktail historian David Wondrich, batched milk punch dates back three hundred years or more. But, he explains, "Milk Punch in a glass and Milk Punch in a bowl or bottle are two entirely different drinks. In the latter, the cream is deliberately made to curdle and then strained out." That version of milk punch, in contrast to its creamy descendant, appeared clear or nearly clear in the bowl.

In 2003 *Delta* magazine suggested a much simpler, charmingly utilitarian way to mix a batch of milk punch for a crowd. The recipe calls for a gallon jug of milk, poured into a pitcher. In the empty jug, place a cup and a half of sugar, a tablespoon of vanilla extract, and a fifth of brandy. After shaking to dissolve the sugar, pour enough of the reserved milk back into the jug to fill it. The resulting jug-o-punch fits easily into the refrigerator, or into a cooler for easy transport to the tailgate. However you choose to make milk punch, grate nutmeg over each serving. Tapping a sprinkle of pregrated nutmeg from a bottle will do, but breaking out the whole seed and the Microplane is more festive—which is what this drink should be.

SCM

Brandy Milk Punch

BRENNAN'S RESTAURANT in the New Orleans French Quarter is a milk punch mecca. This is their recipe.

GARNISH:
Freshly grated
nutmeg

SERVICE ICE:
Cubed

GLASS:
Rocks

YIELD: 1 (7¼-ounce) cocktail

COCKTAIL:
2 ounces brandy
4 ounces half-and-half*
1 ounce simple syrup (see recipe page 174)
¼ ounce vanilla extract

Place brandy, half-and-half, simple syrup, and vanilla in a shaker. Add ice and shake. Strain into ice-filled glass and garnish with freshly grated nutmeg.

*If half-and-half is too rich for you, replace some or all of it with whole milk.

However you choose to make milk punch, grate nutmeg over each serving.

Rum Milk Punch

THERE'S ALMOST ALWAYS a milk punch on the menu at Olamaie in Austin, Texas. The Bananas Foster at Brennan's restaurant in New Orleans inspired Olamaie bartender Erin Ashford to create this sweet and nutty rum-based riff. She raves about Giffard Banane du Brésil, a liqueur made with cognac and Brazilian bananas. Seeking it out over a generic banana liqueur will elevate the finished drink. If you take a shine to it, Ashford recommends pouring the liqueur over a scoop of ice cream for dessert.

GARNISH:
Benne or sesame
seeds

SERVICE ICE:
Cubed

GLASS:
Rocks

YIELD: 1 (4½ to 5-ounce) cocktail

COCKTAIL:
2 ounces dark rum, such as Cruzan Black Strap
2 ounces whole milk
½ ounce banana liqueur, such as Giffard Banane du Brésil
¼ ounce simple cane syrup (combine equal parts water and
    Steen's cane syrup)
40 drops benne seed tincture (see recipe below)

Combine all ingredients in a shaker, add ice, and shake. Double-strain into ice-filled glass and garnish with benne (sesame) seeds.

BENNE SEED TINCTURE:
5 ounces 151-proof vodka
1 ounce benne oil (available commercially from Oliver Farm, using benne
    seed from Anson Mills; you may substitute sesame oil)

Combine ingredients in a mason jar. Close and steep for 24 hours, then freeze overnight. While oil is frozen, remove by passing tincture through a cone filter.

Harry's Bloody Mary

THERE'S NOTHING SOUTHERN about the origin of the Bloody Mary. Created in the 1920s or early 1930s at Harry's New York Bar in Paris, it became a hangover-soothing hit among American expats and tourists looking to slake their Prohibition-induced thirst. Here in the South, it's a staple of holiday brunches and morning tailgates, fuel for duck hunts and wedding parties.

This recipe, adapted from *Harry's ABC of Mixing Cocktails*, is intentionally smooth and thin. And it omits celery salt, which Harry's son, Andy MacElhone, considered an abomination. If you're in the camp that prefers a Bloody Mary with the texture of vodka-spiked gazpacho, feel free to start with one of today's thicker mixes and doctor it to your taste. If you're in the mood to throw tradition to the wind, try Natural Blonde Bloody Mary mix from Charleston, which takes its lovely light-orange hue from South Carolina–grown yellow tomatoes. Regardless, let's agree to keep the garnishes under control, shall we? Over-the-top garnishing has become a kind of sport at restaurant brunches. We recommend choosing between a lemon and a celery stalk. Leave the cheeseburgers, fried shrimp, and charcuterie on the plate, where they belong.

GARNISH:
Lemon wedge or
   celery stalk

SERVICE ICE:
Cubed

GLASS:
Collins

YIELD: 1 (7-ounce) cocktail

COCKTAIL:
4 ounces good-quality tomato juice
2 ounces vodka
½ ounce freshly squeezed lemon juice
6 dashes Worcestershire sauce
3 dashes Tabasco (or to taste)
Pinch of black pepper
Pinch of salt

Place all ingredients in a collins glass filled with ice.
Stir cocktail to incorporate. Serve with a straw.

Michelada

ONE OF THE FEW non-spirits-based cocktails in this book, you can wrap your head around a Michelada by thinking of it as a beer Bloody Mary. Maggi, a European brand of seasoning, is popular almost everywhere in the world *except* the United States, especially in the Global South. Its liquid seasoning and bouillon are staples of home cooks from India to Nigeria to Mexico. If you've never used it before, check the spice section or international foods aisle of your grocery store.

GARNISH:
Lime wedge

SERVICE ICE:
Cubed

GLASS:
Pint glass or similar beer glass

YIELD: 1 (8¾-ounce) cocktail

COCKTAIL:
4 ounces chilled Clamato (or tomato juice)
4 ounces chilled Mexican lager
½ ounce freshly squeezed lime juice
1 dash Worcestershire sauce
1 dash Maggi liquid seasoning
1 dash Tabasco
2 tablespoons kosher salt
½ teaspoon chili powder

Stir Clamato (or tomato juice), lager, lime juice, Worcestershire sauce, Tabasco, and Maggi seasoning in a mixing glass. Mix salt and chili powder on a small plate. Rub rim of beer glass with lime wedge and dip in salt mixture. Fill glass with ice, add Michelada mixture, and garnish with the lime wedge.

Pimm's Cup

PIMM'S NO. 1 is a gin-based liqueur created by a London bar owner in the mid-1800s. Because of its refreshing, heat-beating qualities, the Pimm's Cup cocktail took off in New Orleans in the 1940s at Napoleon House. Pimm's No. 1 clocks in at a modest 50 proof, or 25 percent alcohol by volume. This makes the Pimm's Cup ideal for session drinking, the grown-up term for day drinking in multiples.

GARNISH:
Cucumber spear
and mint sprig

SERVICE ICE:
Cubed

GLASS:
Collins

YIELD: 1 (8-ounce) cocktail

COCKTAIL:
2 ounces Pimm's No. 1
3 ounces lemonade
3 ounces 7-Up or ginger ale

Place Pimm's and lemonade in an ice-filled collins glass and stir. Top with 7-Up or ginger ale and garnish with cucumber and mint.

The Pimm's Cup cocktail took off in New Orleans in the 1940s.

Stocking the Bar

I MOVED TO OXFORD, MISSISSIPPI, in the summer of 2012. I spent the first month subletting a house from a young English professor who was out of state for the summer. I reminded myself that the location of the house, just three blocks from the downtown Square, made up for the fact that the professor, an avid cyclist, had left his sweat-stained jersey hanging in the bathroom—a sort of reverse air freshener.

Soon enough my furniture arrived from North Carolina, and I began to settle in to my rental house. Meanwhile I had met and gone on two dates with Kirk. I wasn't sure how I felt about his being a decade my senior, but I was impressed when he called, not texted, to ask me out to dinner at Snackbar. Five weeks in Oxford, and I already knew it was my favorite restaurant.

"Of course," I said. "Why don't you come over to my house first for a drink. I've just moved in and I have to tell you, my bar is limited to vodka and bourbon. And Miller High Life in the fridge." Before moving to Oxford, I had learned to appreciate Manhattans, Old-Fashioneds, and craft beer in Chapel Hill. Prior to that, it was PBR in Little Rock. Those days were preceded by 4 p.m. Margaritas on weekdays in Houston (before you judge, know that I was a middle-school teacher). But I rarely got fancy in the solitude of my own home.

That evening I heard Kirk's car pull into the driveway. I looked out the window to see him approaching the front door. In his arms he carried a large cardboard box that looked to be full of something heavy. Had UPS come without my noticing? I opened the door.

Kirk was smiling, pleased with himself. He put down the box. "You said you only had vodka and bourbon, so I decided to have a one-man stock-the-bar party." From the box he pulled fifths of gin, scotch, and rum, then two bottles of wine. I don't even remember what we fixed ourselves to drink before dinner. But I was smitten.

The stock-the-bar story rose to the status of legend in our relationship almost as soon as it happened. As much as it came from a place of generosity, Kirk admits now that he was also stocking the bar for himself, hoping to be invited to my house again. In any case, it worked: Two and a half years later, we were married. And our shared cocktail exploration, at home and on the road, was just beginning. By then Kirk had adopted the Barbary Corsair, a rum Negroni, as his usual on our frequent dates to Snackbar. (In fact, it turned out that these Snackbar dates were a little too frequent. Once we began to track our shared finances, we scaled back to once a month. Okay, sometimes twice.) I favored sauvignon blanc, occasionally switching it up with a rye Manhattan or the Lurleen or a new cocktail from the seasonal menu.

Two nights before our wedding, Kirk discovered pine liqueur in a gin cocktail at the now-shuttered Bellocq in New Orleans. (Thanks to Mississippi's byzantine liquor laws, it took us more than a year to track down a similar product, Dolin Génépy des Alpes, for our home bar.) After the wedding ceremony, I drank wine and champagne on the third-floor balcony at Galatoire's. By the time we cut the cake, I knew I would be too exhausted to venture on Bourbon Street in my wedding dress, new husband in one hand and go-cup cocktail in the other.

There were more discoveries to come. Cynar at Zuni Café in San Francisco on our honeymoon, where we were intrigued by the artichoke on the bottle and asked the bartender to pour us a taste. (After more searching, it too earned a permanent place on our home bar.) There was a coveted taste of watermelon brandy in Charleston, and yellow-tomato Bloody Marys over the bridge in Mount Pleasant. (Three quarts of the mix came home with us.) A white Negroni in Chicago, made with a melon amaro. The makings for Pimm's Cups, carried to college baseball games in a soft-sided cooler and mixed on a picnic table. A collection of bitters that multiplied beyond the confines of the bar proper (or "bar" not so proper, as it was, until recently, a shelf above the microwave). Palomas and Greyhounds at home and in bars, to satisfy our healthy thirst for grapefruit juice. And, more often than not, a beer and a sandwich in a dim pub off the Square on Saturdays, followed by a nap for me and sports on television for Kirk. We even attempted to serve Chatham Artillery Punch at a tailgate one football weekend—an attempt that failed spectacularly when the glass jar of shrub fell to the ground and shattered on the bricks en route to the Grove.

Even if we both reach for a simple glass of wine most nights, we still have plenty of exploring ahead of us. I'm on cocktail sabbatical as I write this, awaiting the arrival of our first child. Kirk has gallantly shouldered the responsibility of drinking for two, and I've added at least a dozen drinks to my own bucket list. I'll get there soon enough. After all, love is a well-stocked bar.

SCM

Gunshop Fizz

THIS PIMM'S CUP VARIATION uses a whopping 2 ounces of Peychaud's bitters. An unorthodox yet refreshing change of pace, it's a cult favorite at Cure in New Orleans, where it was created. The drink takes its name from the building at 437 Royal Street in the French Quarter where Antoine Amédée Peychaud once kept his apothecary. Since 1898 it's been home to James H. Cohen and Sons, a dealer in antique guns, swords, and coins. The deep red color of San Pellegrino Sanbitter soda is similar to that of Peychaud's. Whereas San Pellegrino's citrus-flavored sodas—Limonata, Aranciata, and their siblings—are increasingly available outside major cities, Sanbitter is still hard to find. You can approximate the flavor profile by substituting ½ ounce Campari and ½ ounce soda water.

GARNISH:
Cucumber slice

SERVICE ICE:
Cubed

GLASS:
Collins

YIELD: 1 (6-ounce) cocktail

COCKTAIL:
2 ounces Peychaud's bitters
1 ounce freshly squeezed lemon juice
1 ounce simple syrup (see recipe page 174)
2 whole strawberries, stems removed
3 cucumber slices
3 (1-inch) pieces grapefruit peel
3 (1-inch) pieces orange peel
1 ounce San Pellegrino Sanbitter soda

Place bitters, lemon juice, simple syrup, strawberries, cucumber, and grapefruit and orange peels in a shaker. Muddle well. Set aside for 2 minutes to allow flavors to blend. Add ice, shake. Strain into ice-filled glass, add Sanbitter soda, and garnish with cucumber slice.

Paloma

As popular as a Margarita in Mexico, this refreshing tequila cocktail can be customized to your lowbrow/highbrow desires. Want a quick porch-sitter drink? Toss a pinch of salt in your tequila and lime and top with Mexican grapefruit soda. Want to up your taco-night game? Rim the glasses with salt and replace the Jarritos with 2 ounces of fresh ruby-red grapefruit juice, ½ ounce of simple syrup, and 2 ounces of soda water. Little Donkey in Homewood, Alabama, serves an excellent version with fresh grapefruit juice and agave nectar. Like a Ruby Slipper, a Screwdriver, or a Salty Dog, you can get away with ordering a Paloma at brunch or lunch. A single serving isn't going to end your day. Then again, it's hard to stop at one.

GARNISH:
Lime wheel

SERVICE ICE:
Cubed

GLASS:
Rocks or collins

YIELD: 1 (6½-ounce) cocktail

COCKTAIL:
2 ounces tequila, reposado or blanco
½ ounce freshly squeezed lime juice
Pinch of salt
4 ounces grapefruit soda, such as Jarritos, or more to taste

Place the tequila, lime juice, and salt in the glass. Fill glass with ice and stir. Top with grapefruit soda. Garnish with lime wheel.

You can get away with ordering a Paloma at brunch or lunch.

Ruby Slipper

A GUSSIED-UP JOE COLLINS, or Vodka Collins, enhanced by grapefruit and rosemary. The redder the grapefruit, the better. Created at H. Harper Station in Atlanta, this is a fantastic brunch drink and a refreshing departure from the standard Bloody Mary or Mimosa. Try serving it by the pitcher for a breakfast or luncheon: Combine the grapefruit juice, vodka, and rosemary syrup in a single batch, then top each drink with soda water before serving.

GARNISH:
Rosemary sprig

SERVICE ICE:
Cubed

GLASS:
Collins

YIELD: 1 (6½ to 7-ounce) cocktail

COCKTAIL:
2 ounces freshly squeezed ruby-red grapefruit juice
1½ ounces vodka
½ ounce rosemary syrup (see recipe below)
3 to 4 ounces soda water

Pour grapefruit juice, vodka, and rosemary syrup into a shaker, add ice, and shake. Strain into ice-filled glass, top with soda water, and garnish with rosemary sprig.

ROSEMARY SYRUP
1 cup water
1 cup sugar
3 rosemary sprigs

Place water and sugar in a small saucepan, set over high heat, and bring to a boil. Boil for 3 minutes. Remove from the heat, add rosemary, cover, and steep for 30 minutes. Strain and cool to room temperature. Refrigerate in a lidded container for up to 3 weeks. *Yield:* Approximately 1½ cups

2

Shake It Up
Ramos Gin Fizz

Shake It Like a Polaroid Picture

If you like efficiency and practicality, the Ramos Gin Fizz might not be for you. The nineteenth-century recipe calls for seven ingredients and takes at least three times as long to make as it does to drink. Yet we promise you it's worth the effort, whether you make it at home or order it in a bar. (Bartenders who know how to make one will agree—perhaps grudgingly.)

Henry Charles "Carl" Ramos, who first mixed the concoction in New Orleans in the 1880s, must have liked to watch his employees sweat in the name of customer service. As you know if you've worked behind a bar or experimented in your kitchen, it takes muscle to emulsify dairy in a cocktail. Ditto egg. Combine the two, as in a Ramos Gin Fizz, and you compound the time and effort required to achieve a smooth consistency. Mix a few and you can safely skip Pilates class.

Word spread, and the Ramos Gin Fizz took off. Ramos had to fortify his staff to keep up with demand. As fast as a bartender could mix the gin, citrus, powdered sugar, cream, egg white, seltzer, and orange blossom water over ice, he'd pass the shaker to a "shaker man." By some contemporary estimates, that person would go to town for as long as fifteen minutes before the drink reached its proper consistency: silky, creamy, and blissfully cold. Most of Ramos's shaker men were African American. They probably didn't get the thanks—or the tips—that they deserved. An often-reported statistic claims that during the 1915 Carnival season, thirty-five shaker men worked steadily behind the bar at Ramos's Stag Saloon in what is now New Orleans's Central Business District. Taking turns offered brief moments of respite and kept the Gin Fizzes flowing.

The Ramos Gin Fizz craze flourished until Prohibition. After repeal, the bar at the Roosevelt Hotel claimed the drink as one of its house specialties. You can still sidle to the bar at the Roosevelt and order a proper Ramos Gin Fizz. If you find yourself craving one outside the Crescent City, it might not be as easy to find. Senator Huey Long knew that. In 1935, just a couple of months before he was assassinated, he flew a bartender up from Louisiana to shake Gin Fizzes at a New York City hotel.

Today we know of at least one satellite mecca for the Ramos Gin Fizz: Decatur, Georgia. Kimball House is located in a former train depot at the edge of downtown. As soon as you sit down, order two drinks: a Ramos Gin Fizz, and whatever you want to sip on while you're waiting for the magic to happen. That magic entails nearly half an hour of mixing, shaking, chilling, and setting. Often a pair of bartenders will tag-team the labor. Your server presents the finished drink in the sort of tall, tapered glass used in an old-fashioned ice cream parlor. The foamy head, punctured by a metal straw, rises at least an inch above the rim.

Wherever you drink it, the Ramos Gin Fizz, made properly, is a minor miracle of chemistry, a chance for the bartender to show off her craft, and a vehicle for nostalgia. That first Gin Fizz goes down like the milkshakes you ordered at the soda fountain as a child—only lighter, brighter, and, yes, a little boozy.

SCM

Ramos Gin Fizz

GARNISH:
None

SERVICE ICE:
None

GLASS:
Collins

YIELD: 1 (7-ounce) cocktail

COCKTAIL:

1½ ounces gin

½ ounce simple syrup (see recipe page 174)

½ ounce freshly squeezed lemon juice

½ ounce freshly squeezed lime juice

1 egg white

1 ounce heavy cream

3 drops orange blossom water

2 ounces chilled seltzer

Place all ingredients except soda water in a cocktail shaker without ice. Shake hard for at least 2 minutes. Add ice and shake hard for at least 1 minute. Strain into glass and top with soda water.

It takes muscle to emulsify dairy in a cocktail.

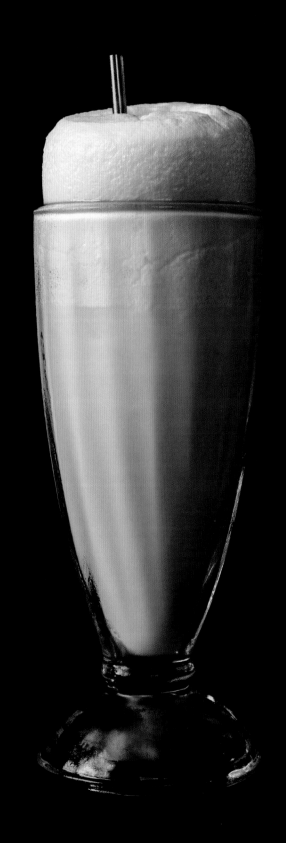

Kimball House Gin Fizz

For the strong of arm (and of patience):

GARNISH:
None

SERVICE ICE:
None

GLASS:
Collins

YIELD: 1 (7-ounce) cocktail

COCKTAIL:
1½ ounces gin
½ ounce freshly squeezed lemon juice
½ ounce freshly squeezed lime juice
¾ ounce simple syrup (see recipe page 174)
¾ ounce heavy cream
1 egg white
3 drops orange blossom water
Seltzer

Place all ingredients except seltzer in a shaker and dry-shake (without ice) for 30 seconds to initially emulsify the egg white and cream into the gin and citrus. Add one 2-inch ice cube and shake vigorously for 1 minute. Add five 1-inch ice cubes and shake vigorously (a strong shake is very important for this drink) for 2 minutes more. Take a chilled collins glass and add a small amount of seltzer to the bottom. Double-strain the Gin Fizz into the glass, allowing the head to rise ½ inch above the glass. Put a straw in the drink, place in the freezer for 5 minutes, then set on the counter for an additional 5 minutes to allow the meringue to set. Gently pour seltzer down the center of the glass, letting the drink rise up an additional 2 inches. (Show out and you will make a mess.) Finish by adding an additional 5 drops of orange blossom water to the top and enjoy. Though this drink takes a while to make, you should consume it within 5 minutes for the best result.

Pendennis Club Cocktail

FOUNDED IN LOUISVILLE IN 1881, the Pendennis Club took its name from the titular character in an 1850 novel by William Makepeace Thackeray. (The character, in turn, was named after a castle built circa 1540 in Cornwall in southwestern England.) The club moved to its current digs in 1928. In the ensuing nine decades it has, among other milestones, begun accepting female members and members of color, developed an erroneous reputation as the birthplace of the Old-Fashioned (more on that later), and given birth to this eponymous cocktail—which, perhaps surprisingly, contains not a drop of Kentucky bourbon. The club itself isn't even sure of the drink's exact history. Today, though, you don't have to be a squash player or a power luncher to enjoy a Pendennis Club Cocktail.

A word about apricot brandy: Since we don't know exactly when this drink was invented, we're not sure what kind of apricot brandy would have been used in the original recipe. Today, real apricot brandy is expensive and hard to find, and it would be too dry in this recipe. Much of what is marketed as apricot brandy and widely available in the United States is actually apricot liqueur. As long as you don't veer too cheap or too sweet (they often go hand in hand), the liqueur is actually the right fit for this drink.

GARNISH:
None

SERVICE ICE:
None

GLASS:
Coupe or
martini glass

YIELD: 1 (3¾-ounce) cocktail

COCKTAIL:
2 ounces gin
1 ounce apricot brandy, such as Marie Brizard Apry
¾ ounce freshly squeezed lime juice
3 dashes Peychaud's bitters

Combine gin, apricot brandy, lime, and bitters in a shaker. Add ice and shake. Strain into glass.

Seersucker

LIKE A SEERSUCKER SUIT, this drink is what you reach for when you need to make an impression but you know the heat and humidity will render you a sweaty mess in a matter of minutes. Created in Oxford, Mississippi—a town that knows heat, humidity, and seersucker—the Seersucker is an indirect tribute to Jim Weems, the longtime manager at City Grocery restaurant. The flavor profile works best with Hendrick's, a Scottish gin infused with rose and cucumber, perfect for warm-weather cocktails.

GARNISH:
Thyme sprig

SERVICE ICE:
Cubed

GLASS:
Rocks

YIELD: 1 (6-ounce) cocktail

COCKTAIL:
2 ounces gin, such as Hendrick's
¾ ounce Cointreau
¾ ounce honey-thyme syrup (see recipe below)
½ ounce freshly squeezed lemon juice
1 ounce soda, seltzer, or sparkling water

Combine gin, Cointreau, syrup, and lemon juice in a shaker. Add ice and gently shake. Pour into ice-filled glass, add soda water, and garnish with thyme.

HONEY-THYME SYRUP
½ cup honey
½ cup water
15 to 20 thyme sprigs

Combine honey and water in a small pot and bring to a slight boil. Remove from heat, add thyme sprigs, and allow to steep for 2 hours. Pour cooled syrup into a glass container (do not remove thyme), cover, and refrigerate. Will keep in refrigerator for up to 14 days.

Daisy Buchanan

A DAISY COCKTAIL is a sour with grenadine or fruit and soda water. Here egg white replaces the soda. Jerry Slater created this drink during his tenure behind the bar at Louisville's Seelbach Hotel. In *The Great Gatsby*, Louisville native Daisy Fay and her new husband, Tom Buchanan, celebrated their wedding with a reception in the Seelbach's Grand Ballroom.

GARNISH:
Lemon twist

SERVICE ICE:
None

GLASS:
Coupe

YIELD: 1 (3½-ounce) cocktail

COCKTAIL:
1½ ounces 80-proof bourbon, such as Basil Hayden's
½ ounce yellow Chartreuse
½ ounce freshly squeezed lemon juice
¼ ounce grenadine
1 egg white

Place the bourbon, Chartreuse, lemon juice, and grenadine in a shaker, add ice, and shake. Strain the cold mixture and return to shaker. Add the egg white and shake until foamy, about 30 seconds. Strain into glass and garnish with lemon twist.

Daisy Fay and Tom Buchanan celebrated their wedding with a reception in the Seelbach's Grand Ballroom.

Nihilist Sour

THIS DRINK IS A refreshing and balanced fizz of whiskey and peach. "Even those who believe in nothing enjoy a sour," says its creator, Greg Best of Atlanta's Ticonderoga Club. Shake until you achieve a foamy texture and a beautiful, creamy orange-yellow color.

GARNISH:
Orange peel

SERVICE ICE:
None

GLASS:
Cocktail

YIELD: 1 (6-ounce) cocktail

COCKTAIL:
2 ounces barrel-proof rye (100-proof or greater)
¾ ounce freshly squeezed lemon juice
½ ounce peach liqueur
⅛ ounce simple syrup (see recipe page 174)
4 dashes cardamom bitters
1 egg white

Place rye, lemon juice, peach liqueur, simple syrup, and bitters in a shaker and shake vigorously for 30 seconds to create a foamy mixture. Add ice and shake again. Strain into glass, squeeze orange peel over the drink, and float peel in drink.

"Even those who believe in nothing enjoy a sour."

Gris-Gris Sour

GRIS-GRIS, or voodoo amulets, ward off evil spirits or conjure magic. Rendered in drink form, this gris-gris is a blend of bourbon, chicory, and smoky syrup that will conjure thoughts of Louisiana. Originally called into service as an extender when roasted coffee beans were in short supply in Louisiana, chicory root stuck around as a flavoring agent and nostalgic practice. Hoodoo Chicory Liqueur is made a few hours north of New Orleans by the Jackson, Mississippi, distillers behind Cathead vodka and Bristow gin.

GARNISH:
Brandied cherry

SERVICE ICE:
None

GLASS:
Cocktail

YIELD: 1 (3½-ounce) cocktail

COCKTAIL:
1½ ounces bourbon
¾ ounce Hoodoo Chicory Liqueur
¾ ounce freshly squeezed lemon juice
½ ounce smoked bourbon-barrel maple syrup (Tippleman's
    makes one; regular maple syrup will do in a pinch)
1 egg white

Place bourbon, chicory liqueur, lemon juice, maple syrup, and egg white in a shaker and shake, without ice, for 10 seconds. Add ice and shake again. Fine-strain into chilled glass and garnish with skewered cherry.

Old Spanish

THIS RECIPE falls into the category of suppressors, low-proof cocktails intended to prevent overindulgence. Paul Calvert, now a co-owner of Ticonderoga Club in Atlanta, took as his inspiration an unintentionally sophisticated practice he began with college friends in Charleston: drinking fortified wine mixed with tonic. The drink's name is a nod to the sherry, which must be produced in Jerez de la Frontera, in southwestern Spain.

GARNISH:
White-grapefruit
or lemon twist

SERVICE ICE:
Cubed

GLASS:
Collins

YIELD: 1 (6-ounce) cocktail

COCKTAIL:
2 dashes Angostura bitters
2 ounces sweet vermouth, such as Cocchi di Torino
1 ounce oloroso sherry
4 ounces tonic water

Fill glass with ice. Add bitters, vermouth, sherry, and tonic water. Stir gently to combine. Garnish with twist.

Suppressors are low-proof cocktails intended to prevent overindulgence.

General's Orders

FOR THOSE SOLDIERS who remained loyal after Valley Forge's terrible winter, General Washington ordered a bonus of a gill (¼ pint) of whiskey and a gill of rum. Based on the Singapore Sling, and using Martha Washington's Cherry Bounce, this cocktail comes from Derek Brown, who often draws on history to inspire the menus at his bars in Washington, D.C.: Mockingbird Hill, Southern Efficiency, Eat the Rich, and Columbia Room. If you're not up for the DIY Cherry Bounce, substitute ¼ ounce Cherry Heering and a dash of Angostura bitters.

GARNISH:
Orange slice and
brandied cherry

SERVICE ICE:
Cubed

GLASS:
Highball

YIELD: 1 (4½-ounce) cocktail

COCKTAIL:
1 ounce aged rum
½ ounce rye whiskey
¾ ounce freshly squeezed lemon juice
½ ounce simple syrup (see recipe page 174)
¼ ounce Cherry Bounce (see recipe below)
1 ounce soda water

Place rum, rye, lemon juice, simple syrup, and Cherry Bounce in a shaker, add ice, and shake. Strain into ice-filled glass, add soda water, and garnish with orange slice and brandied cherry.

CHERRY BOUNCE
2 to 3 pounds fresh sour cherries, pitted, or 2 (15-ounce) cans tart cherries
2 cups brandy
1½ cups sugar
1 whole clove
1 cinnamon stick

Place fresh cherries in a bowl and mash with a potato masher to extract as much juice as possible from the fruit. Strain through a fine mesh strainer, pushing as much juice out of the fruit as possible. Discard fruit pulp or save for another use. (If using canned, drain the fruit, reserving liquid in a medium bowl. Mash the fruit and add any juice to the reserved liquid.

Transfer the liquid to a 2-quart lidded glass jar. Add the brandy and sugar and stir to combine. Refrigerate for 24 hours, stirring occasionally to help sugar dissolve. The next day, bring 2 cups of the mixture to a simmer over high heat. Reduce the heat to maintain a simmer, add the clove and cinnamon stick, and cook for 5 minutes. Cool to room temperature, remove spices, and add back to the remaining mixture. Cover and set aside for 1 to 2 weeks or until desired flavor is achieved. Will keep in airtight container for up to 3 months.

Yield: Approximately 3 cups

Saved by Zero

LIKE A DAISY OR A SOUR, the fix is its own drink category, albeit a lesser-known one. Cocktail historian David Wondrich says that the term is short for "Fix-Up," and he describes it as a "short Punch," cousin to the sour and characterized by a fruity garnish. Jerry Slater's twist on the fix forgoes the fruit garnish in favor of a dose of pineapple syrup. As for the name, it's a nod to British new-wave band The Fixx. You know them from their 1983 hit "One Thing Leads to Another." "Saved by Zero" appeared on the same album, *Reach the Beach*. (If you're unfamiliar, cue up the video on YouTube and bask in the glory of lead singer Cy Curnin's majestic bangs.)

GARNISH:
None

SERVICE ICE:
Cubed

GLASS:
Rocks

YIELD: 1 (3-ounce) cocktail

COCKTAIL:
1½ ounces Tennessee whiskey
½ ounce freshly squeezed lemon juice
½ ounce pineapple syrup (see recipe page 174)
¼ ounce green Chartreuse

Place whiskey, lemon juice, pineapple syrup, and Chartreuse in a shaker, add ice, and shake. Double-strain into ice-filled glass.

New Orleans, Bar City

NEW ORLEANS is lousy with great bars, from shot-and-a-beer Mid City saloons with particleboard walls to venerable Garden District salons with tufted velvet booths and brass chandeliers. Researching and writing this book, we've treated the supremacy of New Orleans bar culture like the tipsy elephant in the room, the obvious truth that no denial can blunt. It's now time for the elephant to dance.

Over the years, the SFA has curated two bartender oral history projects in New Orleans. Through that work, we met Gertrude Mayfield of the buzzer-accessed Mayfair Lounge, Michael Smith of the veranda-fronted The Columns bar, and O'Neil Broyard, the late shepherd of the Saturn Bar, an avant-funk roadhouse with neon lights that recall Saturn booster rockets, a collection of folk art rendered by an itinerant painter, and a back room where bare-knuckle fighters once went toe to toe in a makeshift ring.

Through that work we also came to appreciate how New Orleans bars serve as bunkers and porches, clubhouses and business incubators. Ever present, always inspiring, accommodating any thirst, these are fabled American spaces, where pirates frolicked, madams grew rich, and insurrectionists plotted revolt. They are not places to escape the funk and fecundity of the city. Instead, they are diving boards from which drinkers plunge deep into civic life. Bars here are forums, where unrelated people relate as equals.

It would be easy to categorize New Orleans as a museum of drinking culture, where old-guard tenders pour archaic drinks from historic-register-worthy spaces. To that end, an institution dedicated to cocktail history planted its flag there. The Museum of the American Cocktail displays drinking apparatuses, cocktail monographs, and art nouveau absinthe advertisements.

It's a well-outfitted place, worthy of an afternoon visit. But what make this city our region's best drinking lair are the ways in which cocktail culture here has avoided the mothball treatment, spanning chasms of time, remaining relevant across race and class divides. Before a museum opened to preserve its past, New Orleans was already staging nightly cultural expositions, in which pre-Prohibition drinks like Sazeracs were not marvels retrieved from the vault but everyday quaffs, served in plastic go-cups and faceted crystal alike.

Yes, there were dark years. Honest absinthe was illegal for a few decades. Proper Gin Fizzes were once hard to come by. Even during that downturn, block-chipped ice remained the customary chiller for three-finger cocktails, and syrups like orgeat that fell out of favor elsewhere remained back-bar standards. Today tenders at bars like Arnaud's French 75 and Cure proudly carry on the traditions they inherited. They do so out of respect for the women and men who came before them and the clientele that claims bar perches each night.

Instead of a museum dedicated to past glories now in decline, we think of New Orleans as a living history exhibit, where old informs new and culture is an ongoing process, batched and garnished nightly. Here, Uptown bars like Snake and Jake's Christmas Club Lounge pour tequila shots until sometime after sunrise, which is about the same hour when barmen at Brennan's in the French Quarter begin to stir brandy-goosed milk punches. In New Orleans, the pleasures and vices of drink get their best exposition, and the elephant in the room sometimes shimmies across the bar in a tutu.

JTE

Risk

At Saturn in Birmingham, bar manager Steva Casey creates cleverly themed menus that change with the seasons. This gin-based cocktail comes from a Saturn menu in which all of the drinks were named after classic board games. Casey explains that this recipe merited the name Risk because, initially, it might fall outside the comfort zone for some customers. For this drink she favors Bristow gin from neighboring Mississippi.

GARNISH:
Lemon peel

SERVICE ICE:
Single large cube

GLASS:
Rocks

YIELD: 1 (2½-ounce) cocktail

COCKTAIL:
1½ ounces gin, such as Bristow
½ ounce Pimm's No. 1
½ ounce jasmine tea syrup (see recipe below)
2 dashes celery bitters, such as Bittermens

Combine all ingredients in mixing glass with ice. Stir and strain into rocks glass over large ice cube. Garnish with lemon peel.

JASMINE TEA SYRUP
1 cup sugar
1 cup water
2 tablespoons jasmine tea leaves

Combine all ingredients in a saucepan and simmer over medium heat until sugar is dissolved. Strain out tea leaves and discard. Store syrup in a sealed glass container in the refrigerator.

3

Top with Bubbles
French 75

I'll Take My Chances

You will never make my favorite drink incorrectly. I will not allow that
to happen. Not in a didactic, bossy, or witchy way—I don't have printed
recipe cards in my purse or the proportions tattooed up my forearm.
I'm just fully prepared to enjoy whatever version of a French 75 you'd
care to serve me. Life is too short to be doctrinaire about my cocktails or
deliberately set myself up for disappointment. At least not when there are
bubbles to be drunk.

I have a thing for this drink. It hits all my buttons: tart (usually lemon
juice, sometimes lime), sweet (sugar, simple syrup, or orange liqueur),
fizzy and fancy (champagne or a reasonable analogue), strong—and here's
where it gets interesting. By the reckonings of most old-timey bar books
and fellas with wax-tipped moustaches, the hard booze used can be either
gin *or* cognac. Either is right, so neither is wrong, and I might as well try
plenty of 'em just to make sure. I love to sip a French 75 in the cool of a
hotel lobby in a city where I've never been before, pair one (or two) with a
rare long weekday lunch that makes me feel like I've thieved an hour from
the gods, or nurse one at a sleek, bland airport bar as my flight time gets
shoved back, and back again.

It's not *just* the drink; it's the conversation and surprise served
alongside it, especially at a place where they're not often ordered. I'm not
a jerk, strolling into a beer hall or a honky-tonk demanding my twee little
beverage. But if I see the makings on the bar, maybe a lightly abused piece
of citrus and a stab at a cocktail list, I'll take my chances.

The French 75 (it's actually the name of a piece of World War I field artillery) is not definitively French. There's much debate over its place of origin. Some say it came into being at Harry's New York Bar in Paris, or possibly the Hotel Chatham down rue Daunou. Others maintain that it came from an American fighter pilot or from Buck's Club in London. Maybe a variation on a Tom Collins or a Champagne Cup, but possibly an upgrade on the popular French combo of cognac and champagne.

Should you be lucky enough to nab an empty stool at Arnaud's French 75 Bar on Bienville Street in New Orleans, Chris Hannah—the bartender who has likely poured more of them than anyone else on the planet—might hand you a four-page, typewritten, imagined conversation with the legendary and long-dead bartender Harry Craddock, wherein they muse over those origin stories.

I don't recommend that. Not at first. Not until you've gotten a few dozen under your belt (not all at once) and fully appreciated the range of expression, the possibilities of the mixological palette that renders a French 75. Because the one Chris will pour you might ruin you for the rest. It starts with a frosted tulip glass. Then Courvoisier vs, simple syrup, and lemon juice, shaken and strained. Then topped with Mumm's Cordon Rouge. Then a twist. Then bliss. Then regret.

When I visited Arnaud's one Easter morning, I chased Hannah's French 75 quickly with a cup of coffee and a massive seltzer, needing to lightly mar the memory. I get to New Orleans frequently, so I'm confident it won't be my last, but knowing it's out there makes me have a bit less abandon in my explorations. Like meeting the love of your life when you're in high school and still have so much misguided kissing, screwing, and crushing to do. I'm not ready to settle down yet. I still have many years of wandering and tippling ahead of me. For now, I know I'll always have that taste of Paris. Or possibly London. And definitely New Orleans.

KK

French 75

SOME COCKTAIL HISTORIANS, including David Wondrich and Jeffrey Morgenthaler, think this drink is simply a Tom Collins that substitutes champagne for soda water. This knowledge does not steal its mysteries.

GARNISH:
Lemon spiral

SERVICE ICE:
Cracked

GLASS:
Collins

YIELD: 1 (5½-ounce) cocktail

COCKTAIL:
1½ ounces gin
½ ounce freshly squeezed lemon juice
½ ounce simple syrup (see recipe page 174)
3 ounces chilled champagne

Place gin, lemon juice, and simple syrup in a cocktail shaker. Add ice and shake. Strain into cracked-ice-filled collins glass. Top with champagne and garnish with lemon spiral. (Alternatively, lose the ice and serve in a champagne flute or coupe.)

Hannah's French 75

CHRIS HANNAH INSISTS this is a French cocktail and therefore cognac, not gin, is the base spirit. He makes them at Arnaud's French 75 Bar in New Orleans, so who are we to argue?

GARNISH:
Lemon peel

SERVICE ICE:
None

GLASS:
Flute

YIELD: 1 (5-ounce) cocktail

COCKTAIL:
1½ ounces cognac
⅓ ounce freshly squeezed lemon juice
¼ ounce simple syrup (see recipe page 174)
2½ ounces chilled champagne

Fill the flute with ice, swirl to chill, dump out ice, and set aside. Place cognac, lemon juice, and simple syrup in a shaker. Add ice and shake. Strain into chilled glass, add champagne, and garnish with lemon peel.

Pasture 75

BETH DIXON created this Blue Ridge–inspired spin on the French 75 at Pasture restaurant in Richmond, Virginia. Instead of sparkling wine, she uses hard cider as a topper. Try a dry varietal like First Fruit or Serious Cider from Foggy Ridge in the hills of southwestern Virginia. You'll need to infuse the bourbon when honeysuckle blooms (in spring or early summer), making this a seasonal drink. Oleo saccharum is a bit of a project, but well worth making for the intense citrus flavor it imparts. Use any leftovers of either in a punch (see chapter 10) or however suits your fancy.

GARNISH:
Orange twist

SERVICE ICE:
None

GLASS:
Flute

YIELD: 1 (6-ounce) cocktail

COCKTAIL:
¾ ounce honeysuckle-infused bourbon (see recipe below)
½ ounce orange oleo saccharum (see recipe below)
¼ ounce freshly squeezed lemon juice
4 ounces dry sparkling cider

Place bourbon, oleo saccharum, and lemon juice in a shaker. Add ice and shake. Strain into glass, add cider, and garnish with orange twist.

HONEYSUCKLE-INFUSED BOURBON
1 cup honeysuckle flowers
1 cup bourbon

Place flowers and bourbon in a glass jar, seal, and set aside at room temperature. Use the freshest white honeysuckle flowers and use a weight inside your jar to keep the flowers submerged and prevent oxidation during infusing. After 1 to 2 days, strain flowers out. Store bourbon in sealed container for up to 1 month.
Yield: 1 cup

ORANGE OLEO SACCHARUM

8 oranges

½ cup sugar

Remove peel from oranges using a vegetable peeler, leaving as much of the white pith behind as possible. Place peels and sugar in a mixing bowl and muddle orange peels with sugar. Cover and set aside at room temperature for 2 hours or up to overnight. Strain out the orange peels and transfer the liquid to an airtight container. Store, refrigerated, for up to 1 month.

Yield: Approximately ½ cup

Howitzer

ANOTHER PIECE OF European field artillery, the howitzer generally fired shells of a larger caliber than 75mm. Similarly, this bourbon-based riff on the French 75 is a bit more potent than its gin- or cognac-based cousin. It first appeared on the menu at Cure in New Orleans in 2009.

GARNISH:
Lemon zest

SERVICE ICE:
None

GLASS:
Cocktail

YIELD: 1 (5-ounce) cocktail

COCKTAIL:
1½ ounces single-barrel bourbon
½ ounce freshly squeezed lemon juice
½ ounce simple syrup (see recipe page 174)
1 dash peach bitters
2 ounces sparkling wine

Place ice in cocktail glass, swirl until glass is chilled, dump out ice, and set glass aside. Combine bourbon, lemon juice, simple syrup, and bitters in a shaker. Add ice and shake. Pour sparkling wine into chilled glass, strain cocktail mixture into glass, and garnish with lemon zest.

Seelbach Cocktail

IN 1995 ADAM SEGER, the bartender at the Seelbach Hotel in Louisville, rediscovered this 1917 recipe for the hotel bar's signature cocktail. That was the legend until late 2016, when Seger admitted he had invented both the recipe and its backstory. His twenty-year ruse might have rankled some cocktail historians, including those who recounted the fictional origin story of the Seelbach in newspaper and magazine articles, and even a handful of well-researched cocktail books. But as far as we're concerned, the lie doesn't detract from the quality of the cocktail. In just two decades it's become a classic in its own right. Don't let those generous dashes of bitters put you off—this is a beautifully balanced drink.

GARNISH:
Orange spiral

SERVICE ICE:
None

GLASS:
Champagne flute

YIELD: 1 (approximately 6-ounce) cocktail

COCKTAIL:
1 ounce bourbon
½ ounce triple sec, preferably Cointreau
7 dashes Angostura bitters
7 dashes Peychaud's bitters
4 to 5 ounces chilled champagne

Combine bourbon, triple sec, and bitters in a cocktail shaker. Add ice and shake. Strain into champagne flute. Top with champagne and garnish with orange spiral.

Fear and Loathing in Louisville

ARE YOU READY to add a swanky new verb to your vocabulary? Here it is: louche. It's what absinthe does when you add water, turning beautifully cloudy. This drink is essentially a Death in the Afternoon, the absinthe-and-champagne cocktail named after Ernest Hemingway's nonfiction tome on bullfighting. In Louisville, Copper & Kings distills absinthe blanche from muscat brandy. The distillery shares a hometown with the late writer Hunter S. Thompson, whose own imbibing took on Papa-like proportions, and then some. Hence this drink's name.

Shaking the absinthe will cause it to louche (there's that new word!), resulting in a gorgeous milky-white cocktail. The cherry garnish is unorthodox for a Death in the Afternoon, but it makes for an enticing visual pop in the bottom of the drink.

GARNISH:
Brandied cherry

SERVICE ICE:
None

GLASS:
Flute

YIELD: 1 (5½-ounce) cocktail

COCKTAIL:
1 ounce absinthe blanche, such as Copper & Kings
4 ounces chilled champagne

Place the absinthe in a shaker. Add ice and shake. Strain into glass, add champagne, and garnish with cherry.

Louche. It's what absinthe does when you add water, turning beautifully cloudy.

Hoisted Petard

"Petard" is an archaic word for a small explosive. The phrase "hoist with his own petard" comes from *Hamlet*. We still use it today when someone falls into his or her own trap. This absinthe-based cocktail might have had the same effect on its creator, Alex von Hardberger of Snackbar in Oxford, Mississippi. But he's not telling.

Crémant d'Alsace, from northeastern France, is a high-quality, reasonably priced champagne substitute. You can use another sparkling wine if you prefer. There's really no substitute for Bénédictine, an herbal liqueur made in Normandy from a secret recipe of twenty-seven ingredients. It gives this drink its lovely, creamy-yellow color.

GARNISH:
Lemon twist

SERVICE ICE:
None

GLASS:
Coupe

YIELD: 1 (5½-ounce) cocktail

COCKTAIL:
1 ounce absinthe
1 ounce dry vermouth, such as Dolin Blanc
1 ounce Bénédictine
Dash of freshly squeezed lemon juice
2 ounces sparkling wine, such as Crémant d'Alsace

Place crushed ice in a coupe, swirl to chill, dump out ice, and set coupe aside. Combine absinthe, vermouth, Bénédictine, and lemon juice in a shaker. Add ice and shake hard. Double-strain into chilled glass, add sparkling wine, and garnish with lemon twist.

Snake-Bit Sprout

THIS PALE GOLDEN COLLINS-LIKE refresher amplifies the floral qualities of the gin. Chamomile was a folk remedy for snakebite, hence the cocktail's name. Don't be scared off by the infusion. It's simple to make, and you can order a package of dried chamomile flowers online.

GARNISH:
Dried chamomile flowers

SERVICE ICE:
Cubed

GLASS:
Collins

YIELD: 1 (4½-ounce) cocktail

COCKTAIL:
1½ ounces chamomile-infused London dry gin (see recipe below)
½ ounce simple syrup (see recipe page 174)
½ ounce pineapple juice
½ ounce freshly squeezed lime juice
1½ ounces dry sparkling cider

Combine the infused gin, simple syrup, pineapple juice, and lime juice in a shaker. Add ice and shake. Strain into the ice-filled glass, add cider, and garnish with chamomile flowers.

CHAMOMILE-INFUSED LONDON DRY GIN
1 cup London dry gin
1 packed tablespoon dried chamomile flowers

Place the gin and chamomile in a glass container, cover, and set aside for 4 hours or up to overnight. Pour the mixture through a fine mesh strainer and store for up to 3 months in an airtight glass container.
Yield: 1 cup

Dance Caves

INSPIRED BY THE SPEAKEASIES of Prohibition, "secret" bars have been trending for at least a decade now. In-the-know drinkers access today's establishments by phone booths, garage doors, basement staircases, even port-a-johns. But what did the original underground bars of the 1920s and 1930s look like? In the foothills and mountains of the South, bar owners sometimes took the "underground" descriptor literally, setting up shop in the region's plentiful limestone caverns. While some cave clubs, or dance caves, as they were often known, flew under the radar, today we know the stories of a few in Tennessee, Alabama, and Arkansas.

If you were a Jazz Age entrepreneur looking to build a club on the sly, a cave had plenty to recommend it. The walls and roof were already in place, for one, considerably reducing construction costs. In general, a club owner only had to wire the space for electric lights and finish the cave's floor. Concrete was a simple option, but some clubs also laid linoleum tile, installed hardwood dance floors, and carpeted entrances. Most of these caves were strategically located: close enough to cities and towns to build a reliable customer base of middle-class patrons, and just out-of-the-way enough to avoid the attention of city police or the expense of city taxes and inspections. In the days before air conditioning, a cave's most attractive feature was its natural temperature regulation. Many caves in the Southeast and Midwest maintain a constant temperature in the sixties year-round. Sure, the air is a little damp, but imagine the pleasure of sipping an illicit gin in a cool, dimly lit space when it's ninety degrees outside, then taking a spin across the dance floor before ordering another round. In addition to the refreshing temperatures and the even more refreshing beverages, something about the caves themselves might have contributed to their appeal. Maybe the underground location subtly encouraged illicit behavior. Before spring break became a phenomenon, it's fun to imagine Prohibition-era Southerners assuring one another, "What happens in the cave stays in the cave."

In the late 1800s and early 1900s, caves played host to more wholesome activities, too. Sometimes property owners would open for summer picnics and parties, charging a modest admission fee and drawing families from nearby cities. Bands would play dance music, and vendors sold barbecue and soft drinks. This practice became an especially popular pastime in Missouri around the turn of the twentieth century.

Situated at the edge of the Cumberland Plateau, Murfreesboro, Tennessee, is home to a network of limestone caves. Over millennia they have been used by every group to inhabit the area, from pre-Columbian Native Americans to twentieth-century revelers. Black Cat Cave functioned as a speakeasy in the 1920s and 1930s. It gained a reputation as a place for drinking, dancing, gambling, and flirting. The club closed after Prohibition. A new generation of Murfreesboro residents learned about Black Cat Cave's past quite recently. In 2014, after looters vandalized the cave, archaeologists from Middle Tennessee State University (MTSU) arrived to assess the damage and made a breakthrough discovery. In the speakeasy days, club owners had covered the cave's natural earth floor with a layer of concrete. When the twenty-first-century vandals broke through the concrete, they gave the MTSU archaeologists an excuse to dig deeper. Professors brought in student volunteers to help sift through the debris. Under the concrete dance floor, the team found a Native American burial site dating back some five thousand years. The men and women swigging contraband beer and twirling to big-band hits had been dancing on ancient graves.

North Alabama had its fair share of cave bars as well, from rough to refined. Between Birmingham and Cullman, Blount Springs thrived as a high-end "health resort" in the late 1800s and early 1900s. Tourists arrived from all over the South to stay at the town's hotel and partake of the sulphur-rich mineral springs. A local entrepreneur recognized the potential and opened a speakeasy in nearby Bangor Cave. The Bangor Café Club offered alcohol, dancing, and gambling during Prohibition. The Blount County sheriff raided the club repeatedly at the behest of the governor, but its owner and its customers were undeterred. While federal prohibition ended in 1933, the state of Alabama did not legalize alcohol until 1937. Blount County stayed dry even after that. The Bangor Café Club persisted as an oasis until a fire destroyed the cave's interior in 1939.

Perhaps the most impressive of the South's dance caves was Wonderland Cave in Bella Vista, Arkansas, tucked in the far northwestern corner of the state, between Bentonville and the Missouri border. Like Blount Springs, Bella Vista was a resort town, offering lakefront accommodations and recreation in the temperate Ozark hills. In 1929 one of Bella Vista's owners, a real estate developer from Dallas, toured Europe with his wife. He decided that what Bella Vista needed was a nightclub like the ones he visited in Paris. Upon his return to Arkansas, he oversaw the building of his Euro-chic vision—in a cave. Wonderland adopted an exotic Eastern vibe that was fashionable at the time, hanging Japanese lanterns and serving chow mein and chop suey at the tables and booths that surrounded the dance floor. On opening night in 1930, some four hundred revelers stepped across the carpeted entrance and bellied up to the marble-topped bar.

The bummer, for the cocktail historian, is that while descriptions and even some contemporary photos survive from the days of dance caves, cocktail lists do not. Perhaps these clubs chose not to list illegal liquor on their menus. Or perhaps the offerings were so straightforward that they didn't merit a cocktail list. Whatever the reason, while we know that scofflaws visited these caves to slake their thirst, we don't know exactly what kind of alcohol they drank. That's a project for one of today's historian-mixologists: a menu that imagines the cave cocktails of the 1920s and 1930s. The Black Cat Cobbler. The Wonderland Punch. The Bangor Bathtub Gin. We'll take an Underground Old-Fashioned, please.

SCM

Cumberland Sour

THE CUMBERLAND RIVER flows through Nashville, home of this refreshing sour from Matt Tocco. Humble ingredients like sorghum syrup, apple cider vinegar, and Tennessee whiskey combine to create an elegant cocktail. It's worth seeking out Muddy Pond sorghum, grown and pressed by the Guenther family in east Tennessee.

GARNISH:
Orange peel

SERVICE ICE:
Single large cube

GLASS:
Rocks

YIELD: 1 (4½ to 5½-ounce) cocktail

COCKTAIL:
2 ounces Tennessee whiskey
½ ounce freshly squeezed lemon juice
½ ounce sorghum syrup, such as Muddy Pond
⅛ ounce apple cider vinegar
1 dash Angostura bitters
1 to 2 ounces Belgian-style blonde ale

Combine whiskey, lemon juice, sorghum, vinegar, and bitters in a shaker. Add ice and shake. Strain into ice-filled glass, top with ale, then squeeze orange peel and add to drink.

The Cumberland River flows through Nashville.

Summer Shandy

AUSTINITES KNOW HOW TO SURVIVE the heat of summer. This shandy from Erin Ashford of Olamaie restaurant is proof. The simplest shandies, a drink category born in 1920s Europe, combine beer and lemon soda. This recipe elevates the shandy to a restaurant-worthy cocktail or a crowd-pleaser at a summer party. Pilsner is a great session beer, explains Ashford. It's light and crisp enough that you can drink more than one without feeling too heavy (or tipsy). Cappelletti is a wine-based aperitivo with a bright red color similar to Campari, but a slightly milder flavor. Aperol, Campari, or the American-made amaro Bruto Americano would all make acceptable substitutes. If you can't find Meyer lemons, add a splash of orange juice to regular lemon juice, or use slightly less lemon juice and slightly more simple syrup.

GARNISH:
Lemon wheel
(Meyer or regular)

SERVICE ICE:
Cubed

GLASS:
Any pint
beer glass

YIELD: 1 (6½-ounce) cocktail

COCKTAIL:
1 ounce Cappelletti aperitivo
½ ounce dry gin, such as Highborn Texas
¾ ounce freshly squeezed Meyer lemon juice
¼ ounce simple syrup (see recipe page 174)
4 ounces pilsner, such as Live Oak Pilz

Combine all ingredients except for pilsner in beer glass. Add ice, then top with beer. Garnish with lemon wheel.

4

Juleps, Cobblers, and Their Kin
Mint Julep

A Julep in Every Hand

The Mint Julep might be the most storied of the cocktails we profile in this book. And the most celebrated—though sometimes, we believe, for dubious or downright distasteful reasons. We consider it our responsibility to lay bare the icky underbelly of this drink and reclaim it in the name of a more inclusive and progressive future for our region's bars. The Mint Julep's origins lie in early nineteenth-century Virginia, most likely. Today it is the official beverage of the Kentucky Derby. It has come to symbolize an antebellum South caricature, both nostalgic and repulsive. If we can come to terms with its history, we might again enjoy this deceptively simple and pleasing drink.

Let's start with that history. The word "julep" comes from the Persian *gulab*, meaning rosewater. For centuries Persians used sweetened rosewater as a compounding agent for medicines. In colonial Virginia, mint became the vehicle that helped medicine go down. The "medicine" of choice at that time was cognac. Or peach brandy. Or maybe rum. You get the point. Since this was a time when drinking was often an all-day exercise, drinkers took juleps in the morning to cure yesterday's hangover and brace for today's struggle. The first written account of the julep occurs around 1803. By 1816, vacationers at White Sulphur Springs in Virginia (now the Greenbrier resort in West Virginia) were buying them for twenty-five cents each or three for fifty cents.

Race goers have likely been buying Mint Juleps at Churchill Downs in Louisville since the track opened in 1875. The two weren't linked as they are today until after Prohibition ended. In 1938 the Mint Julep became the official drink of the Kentucky Derby. Whiskey distillers, eager to make a comeback, used this event to position their booze as the primary ingredient in the true Mint Julep. That was also when *Gone With the Wind* spurred excitement for all things marketed as "Old South."

The Mint Julep became a symbol for a place, the South, and a time, the antebellum era. Marketers leveraged that dark period of our nation's past to sell consumer goods, from pancake syrup to soap to whiskey. The cover of a chapbook produced in 1945 by the Glenmore Distillery of Louisville is emblazoned with an illustration of a white-haired and goateed gentleman in a dinner jacket and string tie. This white "colonel" extends a welcoming hand while standing on his porch beside a tall white column. Next to him is a smiling, jolly black man, obviously a servant, laying down a silver tray of Mint Juleps. The Mint Julep gets commingled in selling the myth of a "gentler time" and a "happy slave." Uncomfortable iconography for any cocktail.

The Mint Julep is, no matter the stories embedded, just a cocktail. The crushed ice that fills the glass is no longer a luxury. No servant class is required to make one, no horse race prompt is needed for us to enjoy one. Many Louisvillians will tell you outright that they only drink one, one day a year. (The ones they drink at the track are premade facsimiles of the real thing.)

Made with care, good bourbon (or cognac), and fresh mint, a julep can be a refreshing reprieve from Southern heat. Or from a bad Tuesday at the office. With a little practice and patience, we can reclaim Mint Juleps from "moonlit verandas" and put them back on the bar where they belong. One bartender doing just that is Alba Huerta, a native of Monterrey, Mexico, who claims the julep at her bar of the same name (yep, Julep) in Houston, Texas. Whoever you are, wherever you live, we encourage you to do the same.

JS

Mint Julep

GARNISH:
Mint sprig

SERVICE ICE:
Crushed

GLASS:
Silver julep cup, or
rocks glass

YIELD: 1 (2½-ounce) cocktail

COCKTAIL:
2 ounces bourbon
½ ounce simple syrup (see recipe page 174)
4 mint sprigs, the largest and prettiest reserved for garnish

Crush ice, in a Lewis bag if possible. Place 3 sprigs of mint and simple syrup in julep cup or rocks glass. Lightly press mint with a muddler to release aromatic oils. Add bourbon and give a quick stir. Fill the cup ⅓ full with crushed ice and stir. Repeat with another third of ice. Finally, pack the last third with ice mounded like a sno-cone. Take reserved mint sprig in one hand and give a light smack to release the aroma. Plant the sprig in one side of the cup. Add 2 small stirrer-type straws, or a small metal straw, right next to the garnish, so that you smell the mint each time you take a sip.

The first written account of the julep occurs around 1803.

First Julep

The first Mint Juleps relied on cognac or, less commonly, rum. This version, a sort of historical reenactment, uses both. If you see a cognac-based julep on a cocktail menu today, you'll likely find the term "antebellum" somewhere in its name. Historically, that's accurate. Unfortunately, though, that modifier has taken on an air of Lost Cause nostalgia among some folk, and for that reason we prefer to keep it on the shelf. What doesn't need to stay on the shelf is this recipe.

GARNISH:
Reserved
mint sprig

SERVICE ICE:
Crushed

GLASS:
Silver julep cup, or
rocks glass

YIELD: 1 (3-ounce) cocktail

COCKTAIL:
2 ounces cognac
½ ounce simple syrup (see recipe page 174), or,
   for richer, a generous ¼ ounce of sorghum syrup
½ ounce aged rum, Jamaican if possible
4 sprigs mint, one reserved

Crush ice, in a Lewis bag if possible. Place 3 sprigs of mint and simple syrup in julep cup or rocks glass. Lightly press mint with a muddler to release aromatic oils. Add rum and give a quick stir. Fill the cup ⅓ full with crushed ice and stir. Repeat with another third of ice. Finally, pack the last third with ice mounded like a sno-cone. Take reserved mint sprig in one hand and give a light smack to release the aroma. Plant the sprig in one side of the cup. Add 2 small stirrer-type straws, or a small metal straw, right next to the garnish, so that you smell the mint each time you take a sip.

Sparkling Julep

THIS SWEET AND REFRESHING JULEP is a lighter take on the original. As you might expect, Alba Huerta, the drink's creator, is an expert on the julep and its variations. She also creates cocktails that nod to Southern history and culture while incorporating global ingredients.

GARNISH:
Mint sprig

SERVICE ICE:
Crushed

GLASS:
Collins

YIELD: 1 (3¾-ounce) cocktail

COCKTAIL:
12 mint leaves
½ ounce turbinado syrup (see recipe page 174)
¾ ounce cognac, such as Pierre Ferrand 1840
2½ ounces chilled champagne, divided

Place the mint leaves and syrup in the collins glass and lightly muddle. Add the cognac and 2 ounces of the champagne and remove the muddler. Add crushed ice and stir for 10 revolutions. Add the remaining ½ ounce of champagne and garnish with mint sprig.

Made with care, a julep can be a refreshing reprieve from Southern heat.

Oregano Cobbler

THIS SAVORY COCKTAIL is a play on the classic Sherry Cobbler, a nineteenth-century cocktail of fortified wine, sugar, and fruit served over cracked ice. This drink contains all of those elements, but it flips the script from sweet to savory, explains Alba Huerta. The herbal and mineral characteristics from the bianco vermouth, gin, and oregano blend beautifully to make a refreshing and light aromatic cocktail.

GARNISH:
Oregano sprig

SERVICE ICE:
Crushed

GLASS:
Rocks

YIELD: 1 (3-ounce) cocktail

COCKTAIL:
2 small sprigs of fresh oregano
1 ounce bianco vermouth, such as Carpano Bianco
¾ ounce London dry gin
¾ ounce fino sherry syrup (see recipe below)
¼ ounce freshly squeezed lemon juice

Place all ingredients in a cocktail shaker, add ice, and shake. Strain into crushed-ice-filled rocks glass. Garnish with oregano sprig and straw.

FINO SHERRY SYRUP
2 cups white granulated sugar
12½ ounces fino sherry

In a nonreactive pot, dissolve sugar in sherry and reduce by half at a slow simmer. Once cooled, it is ready for use and will keep for several weeks in the refrigerator.

Ticonderoga Cup

THE TICONDEROGA CLUB is a real Atlanta bar named after a fictional eighteenth-century drinking society. You don't have to be in on the joke to enjoy its signature cocktail, the Ticonderoga Cup, which is something of an amped-up cobbler.

GARNISH:
Mint sprig

SERVICE ICE:
Crushed

GLASS:
Mug or julep cup

YIELD: 1 (4½-ounce) cocktail

COCKTAIL:
1½ ounces aged English-style rum, such as Smith & Cross
1 ounce cognac
½ ounce oloroso sherry
½ ounce freshly squeezed lemon juice
½ ounce pineapple syrup (see recipe page 174)

Place the rum, cognac, sherry, lemon juice, and pineapple syrup in a shaker. Add ice and shake. Strain into ice-filled mug and garnish with mint.

Ice, Ice, Baby

THE YEAR IS 1820. On an August evening in New Orleans, you stroll along the waterfront, taking in the sights and sounds of the steamships, trying to catch a breeze. No such luck. You descend back into the city, walk a few blocks into the Vieux Carré, and duck out of the warm, wet air and into a coffee shop. Your brandy arrives, and you take a sip. It's room temperature. You down it quickly, and you're well into your second before you begin to forget how hot you are. Such was the plight of the American drinker well into the nineteenth century.

Think of the ways Southerners cool off in the summer. Air conditioning aside, most methods call for rocks: Iced tea. Gin and tonic. A cold beer. (No, we're not talking about pouring your beer over ice. But let's agree that beer is most refreshing when pulled, sweating, right from an ice-filled cooler.) The early days of the cocktail were the dark, hot days before ice. There were exceptions. The Governor's Palace at Williamsburg, Virginia, operated an icehouse by the 1760s, and George Washington's Mount Vernon ran one by 1784. Charleston, South Carolina, was early to the ice party, at least for its latitude. The city's first icehouse opened in 1798 (but folded two years later). In 1802 then-president Thomas Jefferson built a massive underground icehouse, insulated with stone, at his Monticello estate.

In colonial America, conventional wisdom held that drinking a cold beverage on a hot day could deliver a dangerous, even fatal, shock to the system. Warm beverages, on the other hand, cooled the body from the inside out by causing perspiration. This belief seems to have held on until the late eighteenth or early nineteenth century. Once Americans came to appreciate the luxury of a frosty drink, they devised ways to harvest, transport, store, and distribute ice in bulk. Ice was—sorry, we can't resist—a hot commodity. And Frederic Tudor of Boston was its kingpin.

Tudor joined forces with the inventor of an ice plow that could trim blocks of the stuff from ponds. Before long he shipped ice from New England to such sweltering international destinations as Martinique and Calcutta. He also shipped domestically to the humid coastal cities of Charleston, Savannah, and New Orleans. Tudor owned the icehouses in all of these cities, ensuring control of his product and its profits from departure to arrival. What in the world could keep the blocks from melting during months on the open seas? Humble sawdust, it turned out.

Meanwhile on the Gulf Coast, John Gorrie, a physician in Apalachicola, Florida, saw ice as a solution when yellow fever struck the port town. At the time, doctors didn't know that mosquitoes transmitted the disease. Gorrie noticed a correlation between hot weather and yellow fever outbreaks. He began tinkering, searching for a way to bring cooling relief to his fever patients. At first he created an apparatus that used melting ice to cool the surrounding air. Needing more ice, he came up with a way to produce the ice itself. In the summer of 1847, Gorrie's machine was put to an arguably less humanitarian use: It produced enough ice to chill wine for a local banquet. Gorrie received U.S. and British patents for artificial refrigeration, but he was never financially successful. He was convinced that Frederic Tudor was to blame.

$$\ell\ell\ell$$

It was at least 1830 before ice found its way into the Southern cocktail with regularity. During that decade, ice became associated with the Mint Julep. The two would become inseparable. Those early crushed-ice-packed Mint Juleps, sometimes billed as "hailstorm juleps" on bar menus, were novelties. Without the crushed ice, today's Mint Julep would consist of a sad couple of ounces of bourbon—sweet and minty, but hardly worthy of the silver cup.

By the mid-nineteenth century, you could patronize a decent bar in most American cities and expect your cocktail to be ice cold, served on the rocks or shaken to chill. Ice cracked the cocktail landscape open. It changed the taste profile and mouthfeel of existing drinks and inspired scores of new ones. It required new tools and fostered new techniques. Icehouses delivered ice in large blocks, leaving bartenders to break and shape it. Depending on the demands of the drink, a mixologist (yes, that was a contemporary term) might crack the ice into lumps, crush it with a mallet, or shave it as fine as snow. Since it's hard to dissolve sugar in an icy drink, ice also compelled a shift from cubed or granulated sugar to syrups.

On the other side of the bar, patrons got a new toy: the straw. Many drinkers today shun the straw, but when they first appeared, metal straws were a chic cocktail accessory and something of a medical necessity. "The state of nineteenth-century dentistry dictated that if at all possible the stuff be kept away from direct contact with people's teeth," David Wondrich writes of ice-filled drinks. Aside from a sensitive tooth or the odd cold-induced headache, the only contemporary downside of ice is trying to sip the last of the liquid in your drink as an avalanche hits you in the face. We've all been there. Bartenders, an observant species, recognized this almost as soon as they began serving cocktails over ice. To save their customers that ice-in-the-nostrils embarrassment, they shook or stirred the ingredients over ice, then strained them into a separate glass and served them up. The resulting cocktail was pleasantly cool and went down smoothly, often prompting the customer to order another one. Maybe that was the barkeep's strategy all along.

A century after ice became essential in cocktail bars, makers of home refrigerators began to fit their freezer compartments with automatic ice makers. Today most of us take a freezer bin full of ice cubes for granted. For the most dedicated home mixologists, that's not good enough. Boil water before freezing to minimize cloudiness. And fill silicone molds of various sizes and shapes for perfectly cubed or spherical specimens. If you're an overachiever, order a canvas bag and a wooden mallet for crushing your own ice. Honestly, you don't have to. Yes, the recipes in this book specify the best kind and quantity of ice for making each drink. Yes, one big hunk dilutes the drink more slowly than lots of little cubes, and yes, those perfectly clear orbs are quite pretty. Really, though, this is about personal preference and taste. We're not looking over your shoulder. Ice is a choice we now exercise freely and, for the most part, cheaply. It's an indulgence our man in 1820s New Orleans could not have conceived.

Lowcountry Julep

SPIRITS GURU DAVID WONDRICH firmly believes that Southern distillers need to get busy with rice. Maybe South Carolinian David Shields, the scholar who helped bring back Carolina Gold rice, is the man to help them. Until then, Wondrich recommends making this drink with Kikori, a Japanese blend of three-to-ten-year-old pure-rice shochu. Light, smooth, and mellow, Kikori has what Wondrich praises as a "not-unpleasing, if odd, hint of Asian fungal fermentation." In keeping with the drink's name, Wondrich floats Madeira on top as a nod to colonial Charleston's beverage of choice.

GARNISH:
An "obnoxious forest of mint"

SERVICE ICE:
Crushed

GLASS:
Collins or julep cup

YIELD: 1 (4-ounce) cocktail

COCKTAIL:
2 teaspoons sugar
2 teaspoons water
5 to 6 fresh mint leaves
3 ounces rice whiskey, such as Kikori
¾ ounce Madeira

Stir sugar and water together in the glass. Add mint leaves and press lightly with a muddler. Fill glass with crushed ice. Add rice whiskey and stir. Top with Madeira. Garnish with mint sprig and serve with a straw.

Absinthe Frappé

THIS CLASSIC COCKTAIL was popular in New Orleans before absinthe was banned in 1912. One ounce of booze may not seem like a lot, but most absinthe is bottled between 100 and 120 proof. The anisette enhances the anise flavor of the absinthe without taking the alcohol to a place of excess. And the mint leaves add an extra herbal dimension. Now that absinthe is legal again, this refreshing drink is poised to make a comeback. If you're a lover of black jelly beans, this might become your new signature cocktail.

GARNISH:
None

SERVICE ICE:
Crushed

GLASS:
Absinthe

YIELD: 1 (3-ounce) cocktail

COCKTAIL:
1 ounce absinthe
¾ ounce chilled water
¼ ounce anisette
8 to 12 mint leaves
½ ounce seltzer or sparkling water

Fill an absinthe glass with crushed ice. Place absinthe, water, anisette, and mint in a shaker, add ice, and shake. Double-strain into ice-filled glass. Top with more ice and seltzer or sparkling water.

Most absinthe is bottled between 100 and 120 proof.

Bufala Negra

JERRY SLATER created this drink in 2007, as the cocktail renaissance gathered steam. Some of his customers were initially put off by the idea of balsamic and basil in their bourbon. A decade later, shrubs and drinking vinegars are popular, and herbs of all kinds get play with booze. Jerry's network of tipsters has reported spotting this well-balanced drink on menus from Brooklyn to Oakland to Australia.

GARNISH:
Basil leaf

SERVICE ICE:
Cubed

GLASS:
Old-fashioned

YIELD: 1 (5½-ounce) cocktail

COCKTAIL:
½ ounce balsamic syrup (see recipe below)
5 basil leaves, divided
1 brown sugar cube
1½ ounces bourbon, such as Buffalo Trace (get it—"bufala"?)
2 ounces good-quality ginger beer, such as Blenheim's hot (look for the red cap)

Place the balsamic syrup, 4 basil leaves, and the sugar cube in a shaker and muddle until sugar dissolves. Add bourbon and ice and shake. Strain into ice-filled glass, add ginger beer, and garnish with remaining basil leaf.

BALSAMIC SYRUP:
¼ cup brown sugar
¼ cup water
¼ cup balsamic vinegar

Place brown sugar, water, and balsamic vinegar in a small saucepan set over medium heat. Cook, stirring continually, until the sugar dissolves, 4 to 5 minutes. Transfer to a glass container and refrigerate, uncovered, until cool. Cover and refrigerate for up to 1 month.
Yield: Approximately ½ cup

Bourbon Crush

DESPITE ITS LOCATION on Franklin Street, the main drag alongside the University of North Carolina campus in Chapel Hill, the Crunkleton is not a college bar. It's not the place to go for a Miller Lite, a Jaeger Bomb, or a vodka-cranberry. Thank goodness for that. It is a place that takes its craft cocktails seriously, a place for adults or, occasionally, for graduate students learning the stations of the cocktail cross, from Old-Fashioneds to Manhattans to French 75s. Don't mistake the bar's membership requirement for stuffiness or exclusivity: An archaic state law requires drinking establishments to call themselves private clubs if they don't sell food. Once you pay your $5 and sign in, Gary Crunkleton and his bowtied staff will welcome you with a stiff drink, emphasis on the "stiff." This sweet, refreshing Crunkleton recipe is a rendition of an old-timey smash, a sibling of the julep.

GARNISH:
Fresh blackberry
or other in-season
berry

SERVICE ICE:
Crushed

GLASS:
Rocks

YIELD: 1 (4½-ounce) cocktail

COCKTAIL:
2 ounces bourbon whiskey
½ ounce prepared lemon curd
½ ounce ginger syrup (see recipe page 174)
½ ounce freshly squeezed lemon juice
½ ounce cane syrup

Combine bourbon, lemon curd, ginger syrup, lemon juice, and cane syrup in a shaker. Add ice and shake. Strain into ice-filled glass and top with a fresh berry.

Bill Smith's Shortcut Mint Julep

YOU'LL FIND THIS RECIPE on the drink menu at Crook's Corner in Chapel Hill as Crook's Frozen Mint Julep. It's been there for years and works especially well as a dessert drink, perhaps with an order of meringue-topped banana pudding or a slice of Atlantic Beach lemon-lime pie. More recently, this concoction has earned pride of place at the annual Southern Foodways Alliance Fall Symposium, where it is drunk before the opening supper. This drink is not meant to be an elegant sipper. It's as affable and unassuming as Crook's Corner chef and longtime SFA member Bill Smith. Feel free to use a spoon, a straw, or a finger to achieve your desired consistency as the sorbet melts into the bourbon.

GARNISH:
Mint leaf

YIELD: 1 (3½-ounce) cocktail

COCKTAIL:

SERVICE ICE:
None

1½ ounces bourbon (Crook's Corner uses Rebel Yell)
1 small (2-ounce) scoop mint sorbet

GLASS:
Rocks (or clear plastic party cup)

Pour bourbon into glass. Top with a scoop of mint sorbet and garnish with a mint leaf.

This concoction has earned pride of place at the annual Southern Foodways Alliance Fall Symposium.

5

Have Fun with Your Drink
Hurricane

Here Comes the Story of a Hurricane

"Pour me something tall and strong. Make it a Hurricane before I go insane. It's only half-past twelve, but I don't care: It's five o'clock somewhere," country boy Alan Jackson and beach-rock icon Jimmy Buffett sing in their 2003 paean to afternoon drinking. The drinks that populate this chapter, including the Hurricane itself, encourage you to take yourself less seriously. (We're not saying you have to cut out of work early, don a pair of flip-flops, and cue up a playlist of dubious country-pop. You decide where to draw the line.)

The Hurricane is virtually inseparable from Pat O'Brien's, the French Quarter bar at which it was invented. The drink began as a way to sell off surplus rum. During World War II, when the federal government limited the output of domestic distilleries and funneled most of their production toward the war effort, whiskey was hard to come by. Caribbean rum, on the other hand, flowed freely to the mainland. Importers required bar owners to purchase several cases of rum to get just one case of whiskey or scotch. The bar owners didn't mind too much. Some began to look for creative ways to get the extra rum off their shelves and into their customers.

In 1933, one day before the Twenty-First Amendment repealed Prohibition, Pat O'Brien opened his French Quarter bar. He and his co-owner, Charlie Cantrell, dreamed up the Hurricane around 1940. O'Brien wasn't the first to name a cocktail after the meteorological phenomenon, but Pat O's almost certainly originated the potent, sticky-sweet red punch we know as a Hurricane today. The recipe called for a hefty four ounces of rum, topped with a blend of passion fruit and citrus juices, served over ice and garnished with fruit.

Shelly Oechsner Waguespack, the third generation of Oechsners to manage the bar, says the drink actually takes its name from the tall, curvaceous, footed glass, similar in shape to a hurricane lantern, in which it has been served since the beginning. At the dawn of the Hurricane era, she explains, O'Brien and Cantrell would ask comely young women to circulate around the patio with Hurricanes in hand, offering tastes of the exotic new drink to male patrons. By the 1950s it was a proto-tiki hit.

In the 1960s, Bourbon Street began to cater to tourists and locals who wanted to stroll the Quarter. In 1967, Bourbon Street go-cups began fueling a new kind of Crescent City flaneur. Four years later, the street closed to car traffic. Nearly a half century later, Bourbon is still packed with pedestrians, some walking straighter lines than others. Through it all, Pat O's has thrived, thanks in large part to its signature drink. Unless you order your drink to go or request a plastic cup, your Hurricane will be served in the namesake glass. And, unless you specify otherwise, you'll pay for that glass. For each Hurricane ordered at the bar or on the patio, Pat O's tacks on a glass surcharge to the base price. (So many tourists walked out with the glasses as souvenirs that it just made sense to sell the vessel along with the drink.)

While the glass has stayed the same, its contents have not. Today, bartenders add rum and ice to each glass and then use a clawlike nozzle behind each of the bar stations to dispense juice mix from a central tank, filling three glasses at a time. The bartender garnishes each with an orange slice and a maraschino cherry. Thanks to this assembly line, Pat O'Brien's turns out half a million every year. That's not counting the Pat O'Brien's franchises at the San Antonio River Walk and Universal Orlando. If you can't make it to one of these locations, you can purchase Hurricane mix by the liter online or at many liquor stores. Mix with care, though: Four ounces of rum is twice the strength of your average cocktail, and your backyard is a far cry from Bourbon Street.

SCM

Hurricane

For the history buffs, New Orleans bartender Chris Hannah has imagined an approximation of the original Hurricane. It's a little fresher and a little lighter than today's prefab version, with half the rum of Pat O's recipe. It was a hit with the crowd at the SFA's 2015 Summer Symposium in New Orleans.

GARNISH:
Orange or lime wheel

SERVICE ICE:
Cubed or crushed

GLASS:
Hurricane

YIELD: 1 (4-ounce) cocktail

COCKTAIL:
2 ounces full-bodied rum, such as Appleton Estate Signature or Bacardi 8 Años
½ ounce freshly squeezed orange juice
¾ ounce freshly squeezed lime juice
½ ounce passion fruit syrup (store-bought or homemade)
¼ ounce grenadine

Place all ingredients in a cocktail shaker. Add ice and shake. Strain into ice-filled glass and garnish with orange or lime wheel.

The Hurricane began as a way to sell off surplus rum.

Classic Daiquiri

DON'T UNDERESTIMATE THIS CLASSIC. The recipe is deceptively simple, like an Alice Waters peach-on-a-plate. But when you use good rum, shake hard, and consume cold, you get a magical sum. Think of this recipe as a mother sauce for the other sours in this book.

GARNISH:
None

SERVICE ICE:
Cubed

GLASS:
Cocktail

YIELD: 1 (3-ounce) cocktail

COCKTAIL:
2 ounces white rum
½ ounce freshly squeezed lime juice
½ ounce simple syrup (see recipe page 174)

Place rum, lime juice, and simple syrup in a cocktail shaker. Add ice and shake. Strain into glass.

Creole Crusta

JUST LIKE GREAT FOOD, a great drink should appeal to the eyes as well as the palate. The rim of the glass is encrusted with sugar and benne seeds, and the cocktail glass itself is lined with the whole peel of a lemon. This is a spicy rum version of the classic brandy crusta, first shaken in 1850s New Orleans.

This is probably not a drink for which you have all of the ingredients on your bar or in your fridge already. But before you turn the page in favor of something easier, we'll let you in on a secret: Our recipe tester selected the Creole Crusta, unprompted, as her favorite in these pages. It was also a hit at our photo shoot, where the editors, photographer, and stylist patiently waited to get the right shot, and then pounced on the drink. If a sweet-salty-spicy flavor profile is your thing, this cocktail pushes all those buttons.

GARNISH:

1 tablespoon toasted
   benne seeds
1 tablespoon turbinado
   sugar
Peel of 1 whole lemon

SERVICE ICE:

None

GLASS:

Coupe

COCKTAIL:

1½ ounces Demerara rum, such as El Dorado 5 Year
¾ ounce chili-infused Clément Créole Shrubb (see recipe below)
½ ounce turbinado syrup, or substitute simple syrup (see recipes
   page 174)
½ ounce freshly squeezed lemon juice
2 dashes dandelion bitters (yes, commercial versions exist)

To prepare the glass, take two shallow bowls, mix the benne seeds
and sugar in one, and place some water in the other. Inverting the
glass, dip the rim first into the water and then into the benne seeds
and sugar, gently turning to coat the rim. Turn the glass upright and
line with the whole lemon peel.

Combine the rum, infused Clément Créole Shrubb, turbinado
syrup, lemon juice, and bitters in a shaker. Add ice and shake.
Fine-strain into prepared coupe.

CHILI-INFUSED CLEMENT CREOLE SHRUBB
1 cup Clément Créole Shrubb orange liqueur
¼ teaspoon red pepper flakes

Place the liqueur and pepper flakes in a glass
container, cover, and set aside for 4 hours or up
to overnight. Pour the mixture through a fine
mesh strainer and store the infusion for up to 3
months in an airtight glass container.
Yield: 1 cup

The Moviegoer

CHRIS HANNAH, the New Orleans bartender, has a thing for Walker Percy. Happily, though, this cocktail is bright and refreshing, with none of the melancholy of Binx Bolling in Percy's *The Moviegoer*.

GARNISH:
Orange peel

SERVICE ICE:
None

GLASS:
Cocktail

YIELD: 1 (3½-ounce) cocktail

COCKTAIL:
1¾ ounces gin
½ ounce freshly squeezed lemon juice
½ ounce orange liqueur, such as orange curaçao
⅓ ounce amaro, such as Averna

Place ice in cocktail glass, swirl to chill, dump the ice, and set glass aside. Combine gin, lemon juice, orange liqueur, and amaro in a shaker. Add ice and shake. Strain into glass, squeeze orange peel over glass, and garnish with peel.

This cocktail is bright and refreshing.

Virginia Creeper

THIS DRINK IS INSPIRED by the Caipirinha de Uva, a spinoff of the Brazilian national drink that adds muddled grapes to the basic Caipirinha recipe of cachaça, lime, and sugar. Muscadine grapes are native to the Southeast. Look for large, dark-purple beauties at your farmers' market in September and October. (Green scuppernongs would also work in this recipe.) The cardamom bitters add warmth to the sweet-tart flavor profile.

GARNISH:
None

SERVICE ICE:
Ice from shaker

GLASS:
Rocks

YIELD: 1 (3½-ounce) cocktail

COCKTAIL:
4 muscadine grapes, halved and seeded
½ ounce simple syrup (see recipe page 174)
2 ounces honeysuckle vodka, such as Cathead
½ ounce freshly squeezed lemon juice
2 dashes cardamom bitters, such as Scrappy's

Place muscadines and simple syrup in a shaker and muddle until fruit releases its juice. Add vodka, lemon juice, bitters, and ice and shake. Pour entire contents of shaker into glass.

Rum: The Original Southern Spirit

RUM ISN'T FOR EVERYONE. At least, that's what some people believe. If Captain Morgan ever did your college self wrong, you're excused for feeling nervous around the stuff. Maybe you just haven't met the right rum. Maybe you need to get to know it a little better; learn where it comes from, how it got here, and who its friends are. Rum has been a staple of the Southern bar for much longer than you might think.

"Rum is the history of America in a glass. It was invented by New World colonists for New World colonists," writes Wayne Curtis. Curtis is talking about Caribbean sugar planters and colonial North Americans. Barbados, an island on the southeastern flank of the Caribbean, was at the forefront of early rum production. Mount Gay, in the Barbadian capital of Bridgetown, is the world's oldest continually operating distillery—in operation since at least 1703, and possibly as early as 1663. An English visitor to Barbados in the mid-1600s recalled that his host served him "Kill-Devil," an early term for rum.

When the British first colonized the West Indies, they didn't set out to make rum. Sugar was the first order of business. The industry left tons of waste, in the form of bagasse (spent cane) and excess molasses. Sugar planters figured out that the dregs of sugar production could be distilled into a potent alcoholic spirit. Potent, but definitely not refined. Early on, no rules governed which components of the sugar process could be used in rum making. Anything that could go into the still was fair game. Curtis calls rum "the distilled essence of fermented industrial waste." Unaged Barbados rum was essentially cane moonshine.

Colonists on the North American mainland developed a thirst for that rum despite its godawful taste. In the first half of the 1700s, 90 to 100 percent of Caribbean rum not consumed on the islands went to North America. (British markets came later.) If a colonial tavern stocked one hard liquor, it would be rum. American settlers had begun home-brewing beer and cider practically as soon as they got off the boat, in part because they were leery of fresh water. Rum packed a seductive punch in comparison to their relatively weak cider and beer.

Colonial-era mixology offered an arsenal of strategies for masking rum's repulsive flavor and dulling its bite. Remember, there was no ice to cool that burn in the throat, so these drinks were served at room temperature or heated. The rum drinks at eighteenth-century taverns, like the ones at today's tiki bars, had playful names; Curtis rattles off "a mimbo, a sling, a bombo, a syllabub, a punch, a calibogus, a flip, a bellowstop, a sampson, or a stonewall." Their ingredients weren't fancy, though. The most common mixers were water, sugar, citrus, spices, lager, and egg. And, like the rum drinks at today's bars, too many in one sitting would leave the tippler seeing double. Among a list of some two hundred terms for drunkenness Benjamin Franklin once published in his *Pennsylvania Gazette* newspaper was "been to Barbados."

To be fair, the quality and variety of rum available in the colonies improved over the eighteenth century. Barbados wasn't the only Caribbean island producing the stuff. While Barbadian rum was distilled once, Jamaican rum was double distilled. This made it stronger, more shippable, and therefore more saleable. It was the spirit of choice for the pirates who populated the waters of the Caribbean, coming ashore in places like Port Royal, Jamaica, to provision and carouse. (Yes, there really was a Captain Morgan. Henry was his given name.) Rum improved in flavor during shipping, becoming smoother with a little age. Tavern keepers realized that they could further improve the stuff by letting it rest in the barrel rather than serving it right away.

Enterprising distillers in North America got into the rum game, too. They could cheaply import molasses from the Caribbean and make their own rum, earning a tidy profit. In the 1700s, New England was the center of North American rum distilling, but there were at least a handful of distilleries in the Southern colonies. Rum was popular in port cities like Charleston. It lubricated social visits on Virginia tobacco plantations. Legend has it that, after his death in 1718, the pirate Blackbeard's severed head was cast in silver and made into a bowl used for serving rum punch at a tavern in Williamsburg. You might want to tell that tale yourself at the bar over a rum cocktail one day.

When we talk about rum, it's vital to talk about slavery. The labor of enslaved Africans drove the Caribbean sugar industry and, by extension, the rum industry as well. Wayne Curtis and other historians dispute the Triangle Trade model you might remember dimly from junior-high social studies class. It was said that New England, Africa, and the West Indies formed a triangle of molasses, rum, and slaves. New England imported molasses from the West Indies to make rum. Traders brought the rum to Africa, where they sold it for slaves. They brought the slaves to the West Indies to work on the sugar plantations, and the cycle continued. This model is neat, simple, and easy to sketch on a blackboard. But the reality was probably more complicated.

These trades did take place in the eighteenth century, many times over. It was rare, however, that a single ship completed all three legs of this trade. The triangle gives a lopsided view of trade by volume, too. North American slave traders did sell rum in African ports. But, Curtis points out, only a tiny fraction of New England's rum was exported to Africa. This quantity of rum was negligible in comparison to the number of human beings shipped to the West Indies in bondage or the volume of Caribbean molasses exported to the North American mainland.

By 1800, as domestic whiskey production ramped up, many drinkers developed a preference for bourbon or rye. For the most part, rum was not part of the nineteenth-century evolution of the American cocktail. Rum imports increased again during Prohibition. Thirsty tourists with the means to travel made the short hop from Florida to Cuba, where they sampled the local rum in the form of daiquiris. After Prohibition, a rum surplus flooded American markets. From there, rum suffered a decades-long slide from tiki to tacky.

Today rums run the gamut from spring-break swill to aged sipping spirit with a luxury price tag to match. Much of it comes from the Caribbean and Central and South America. If you're interested in learning about the geographic, stylistic, and age variations on today's rum market, gather some friends and orchestrate a taste test. You can sample *rhum agricole* from the French West Indies, with a pleasantly grassy flavor. Or Jamaican rum, golden with a molasses funk. Demerara rum from Guyana is rich and dark with a flavor profile that plays well in tiki drinks. Domestic options are reappearing, too. Distilleries in Georgia, South Carolina, Tennessee, and Louisiana produce rum, many of them using domestic sugarcane.

We gently suggest that, before you write it off for good, you try at least one of the rum cocktails in this book. We promise they'll banish the memory of Captain and Coke from your brain and your palate.

The Lurleen

THIS BOURBON SOUR is a Brown Derby–Manhattan hybrid named after a dog belonging to Southern Foodways Alliance director John T. Edge and his wife, Blair Hobbs, who in turn named her after the first female governor of Alabama. Jayce McConnell created this drink during his tenure behind the bar at Snackbar in Oxford, Mississippi, where John T. and Blair are regulars, and where the Lurleen has become a house favorite. Even people who think they aren't fans of brown liquor tend to like this drink. The citrus and ginger tone down the bourbon bite. Sweet and sour, it goes down remarkably easily. Pace yourself with a half-dozen Gulf oysters or an order of Parmesan truffle frites before you knock back round two.

GARNISH:
Lemon wheel
Freshly grated
nutmeg

SERVICE ICE:
Single large cube

GLASS:
Rocks

YIELD: 1 (4½-ounce) cocktail

COCKTAIL:
2 lemon wedges
½ ounce turbinado syrup, or substitute simple syrup (see recipes page 174)
5 dashes rhubarb bitters, such as Fee Brothers
3 dashes Angostura bitters
2 ounces bourbon
¾ ounce freshly squeezed grapefruit juice
½ ounce sweet vermouth
½ ounce ginger liqueur

Place lemon wedges, turbinado syrup, and both bitters in a cocktail shaker. Muddle to release juice from lemons. Add the bourbon, grapefruit juice, vermouth, ginger liqueur, and some ice and shake. Double-strain into glass with large ice cube and garnish with lemon wheel dusted with freshly grated nutmeg.

Southern Cola

COULD WE WRITE A SOUTHERN COCKTAIL BOOK without a nod to Jack and Coke? Well, we could have, and we almost did. Jack and Coke and its brother, rum and Coke, haunted us as we debated which recipes to include. Instead we decided on this cocktail from Greg Best, a playful riff on a Cuba Libre (that is, rum and Coke with a squeeze of citrus and a better name). Here amaro replaces the rum, its bitter flavor tempering the Coke's sweetness. The cocktail evolves nicely as the lime cube melts.

GARNISH:
None

SERVICE ICE:
Lime cube

GLASS:
Rocks

YIELD: 1 (6-ounce) cocktail

COCKTAIL:
2 ounces amaro, such as CioCiaro
1-inch cube of frozen lime juice*
4 ounces chilled Coca-Cola Classic

Place amaro and frozen lime cube in a glass. Top with cola and stir.

*Freeze a 3-to-1 ratio of strained lime juice and water. From 12 ounces of lime juice and 4 ounces of water you should get approximately a dozen cubes. They'd be right at home in a gin and tonic, too.

Southern Cola is a playful riff on a Cuba Libre.

I'm Your Huckleberry

As long as we're not taking ourselves (or our drinks) too seriously, we offer one more soda-based recipe. This one takes its name from the famous line uttered by Val Kilmer when he played Doc Holliday in the 1993 film *Tombstone*. Before the real-life Holliday moved to the Wild West and became the stuff of legend, he was born and raised in Griffin, Georgia.

Until recently Cheerwine, a cherry soft drink invented in 1917 in Salisbury, North Carolina, was hard to come by outside its home state. Today it is widely distributed.

Before you write this one off as cloying, give it a chance. The finished drink is a deep garnet red and refreshingly fizzy, the amaro and bitters balancing the Cheerwine. It's perfect for cocktail hour at the O.K. Corral.

GARNISH:
2 brandied cherries on a skewer

SERVICE ICE:
Cubed

GLASS:
Collins

YIELD: 1 (6½-ounce) cocktail

COCKTAIL:
2 ounces rye whiskey, such as Old Overholt (said to be Holliday's favorite)
½ ounce amaro, such as Averna
3 dashes Peychaud's bitters
4 ounces Cheerwine

Combine whiskey, amaro, and bitters in a collins glass. Add ice and stir. Add Cheerwine and garnish with cherries.

Grasshopper

PHILIBERT GUICHET, the owner of Tujague's restaurant in New Orleans, reportedly invented this drink around 1919. This will come as a surprise to drinkers who associate it with 1950s kitsch, or those familiar with the Upper Midwest version, a boozy milkshake in which the crème de menthe and crème de cacao are blended with vanilla ice cream. The original is heavy on sweetness, low on alcohol, and a lovely pale jade green in color. Most barkeeps at Tujague's give the grasshopper a quarter-ounce to a half-ounce float of cognac—because, you know, New Orleans.

GARNISH:
None

SERVICE ICE:
None

GLASS:
Cocktail

YIELD: 1 (3-ounce) cocktail

COCKTAIL:
1 ounce green crème de menthe
1 ounce white crème de cacao
1 ounce half-and-half
¼ ounce cognac (optional)

Place menthe, cacao, and half-and-half in a shaker. Add ice and shake. Strain into cocktail glass. Top with ¼ ounce of cognac, if desired.

Philibert Guichet reportedly invented this drink around 1919.

A Love Letter to Pinkie Master's

"Some places inspire a great thirst in a person." I heard myself speak these words, or a close equivalent, right after I bought a third round for my wife. I try not to mix spirits in one session, but sure, a gin and tonic did sound refreshing. And they had our favorite gin. Never mind that I had started out with a whiskey and a beer, followed by another beer. A gin and tonic was going to extend the amount of time that I could linger.

The place we lingered in was The Original, in Savannah, Georgia. It used to be called Pinkie Master's, and that was the name everyone still used.

Luis Christopher Masterpolis—a.k.a. Pinkie Masters—opened his bar in 1953 as Pinkie Master's Rainbow Room. Over the years, Pinkie Master's, like a lot of great bars, became a political hangout. Jimmy Carter, a good old boy from Plains, was said to have announced his bid for the presidency there. Turns out, Carter did stand on the bar and give a speech, but it was St. Patrick's Day 1978, a year into his term and a year after Luis "Pinkie" Masterpolis passed away.

Over the decades, Pinkie Master's survived many attempts on its life, including a smoking ban and encroaching gentrification. But a stabbing incident in 2015 and the ensuing legal battles over muddy ownership rights looked like they might conspire to shutter the little bar that could. The owners of the building evicted Guy Kirk, who had run it since taking over in 2005 from his mother, Ruby. Then they turned around and re-leased it to a young bartender named Matthew Garappolo. Kirk claimed ownership of some of the bar's most revered objects, including the plaque affixed where Carter had once stood, and the many pictures of local and state politicians who had wandered in (or made calculated appearances under the pretense of wandering in) from the nearby De Soto hotel. He used them to decorate a new Pinkie Master's, which opened in 2016 in Savannah's more touristy river walk area.

The Original suited me fine. I got the feeling the soul of Pinkie would persist beyond mortal squabbles. A rowdy and very hospitable bartender welcomed me. The place still had a great neighborhood dive bar feel. Sure, it had a fresh coat of paint. Some changes were welcome: The Confederate flag, which had hung over the bar since Jim Crow, had been retired to one of those triangular display cases and tucked on a shelf. The interior was still intimate and dimly lit. It was full of regulars and the barkeeps who knew them, and yet an outsider felt welcome immediately. A couple of regulars gave us their barstools. An older man with a thick mustache and the type of short brush cut he had probably maintained since his military days took the last swig off his PBR can. His wife, sporting a closer-to-God bouffant, apparently was not feeling well and had refrained from drinking that night. I knew this because the bartender, the rowdy one who looked like a hair-band lead singer, gave her a hug on the way out and said, "Next time, you and me, shots." She blushed and smiled.

As we settled into their spot, that same bartender took our order, passed it on to his relief, clocked out, and began shooting tequila with friends. Did I mention we were there on a Monday? A few minutes passed with no drinks in sight, and then suddenly our lead singer was back behind the bar, apologizing and pouring and explaining the miscommunication. It was okay. We had been people watching, and I had spotted the jukebox.

That jukebox was a thing of beauty. A nineties CD model with its own alcove. On the wall above it, mounted like a crown, loomed a gilt-framed portrait of David Lee Roth, looking like an S&M Saint Sebastian. I filled the jukebox with dollars because it was packed with everything from Merle Haggard to the Replacements, and because when the selections ended, the off-duty bartender's iPod would start playing eighties heavy metal. This battle raged until I played "The Boys Are Back in Town," and the bartender ran over to show me his original Thin Lizzy pin on his jean jacket.

About this time a group of tourists, at least a dozen, descended. It seemed as though this stop had been preplanned and prepaid. Heavy-metal dude jumped back behind the bar and helped his compatriot get through the rush. Savannah, being the drinking town it is, allows open carry on the streets. The folks were one-and-done and out the door as quickly as they had arrived. Those remaining breathed a collective sigh and went back to their drinks and their conversations.

We were almost finished with our last round and ready to stroll back to our hotel. When it came time to pay, The Original proved its dive-bar bona fides with a one-two punch. They accepted only cash. And the drinks were cheap. My resourceful wife had just enough cash to cover the tab and a nice tip. As we left, we joked that if we ever started a hair-metal cover band, we would call it Fifty Dollars of Fun. As we walked away from the corner of Drayton and East Harris, the breeze and the company were especially pleasant, but I was still thirsty. One day I hope to return for the inexpensive drinks, the jukebox, and the company—that rainbow of humanity at what was once Pinkie Master's Rainbow Room.

J S

6

Stirred and Boozy
Manhattan

Mic Check 2-1-2

This is not a Southern-born drink. Its origins lie not with bourbon but with rye whiskey, of which there were many distilleries in pre-Prohibition New York State. Even its proportions, 2:1:2, evoke the original area code for Manhattan. But this drink, along with the Old-Fashioned and a few others, is a universal passkey to pleasure.

Let's talk about those proportions and what they mean to your cocktail making. Although 2:1:2 might sound like the mic check for a great Southern hip-hop act, like Outkast, you should also think about it like the basic rhythm of a jazz standard, like "Li'l Liza Jane," from which many improvisations can launch. The formula 2:1:2 means two parts whiskey, one part sweet vermouth, and two dashes of bitters. The whiskey in question was originally rye. During Prohibition it might have been Canadian. Until a recent rye revival, bourbon was the usual choice south of the Mason-Dixon Line. Sweet vermouth tempers the heat of the whiskey. A fortified and aromatized wine, vermouth is made by adding alcohol to stop fermentation. Many vermouth producers add herbs, spices, and other ingredients for flavor and aroma. Stirred together on ice, vermouth and whiskey result in a pleasant dilution.

The last "2" in our cocktail Morse code is bitters. Bitters are botanicals dissolved in alcoholic solutions. They began as patent medicines, sold by apothecaries making wild claims about their curative properties. Bitters are now known as flavorful additions to cocktails. The best-known bitters are Angostura, from the islands of Trinidad and Tobago, and Peychaud's, from New Orleans. Angostura gets star treatment in the Manhattan. Think of bitters as the "salt" of the cocktail. In the same way that you wouldn't omit salt from a complex dish, leaving the bitters out of the Manhattan produces a drink less interesting and lacking balance.

Now that you have the rhythm of this classic cocktail, you can improvise the melody. Southern bartenders are doing this today. And a number of them are doing it with local ingredients. Got a new small-batch Tennessee whiskey? Swap it for the rye. Found an amaro made in Charleston from local ingredients? Try it in place of the sweet vermouth. A small company in Atlanta is making bitters? Add three dashes instead of two. Not all riffs on this classic may work, but the research and development sure is fun.

JS

Manhattan

GARNISH:
Maraschino cherry

SERVICE ICE:
None

GLASS:
Cocktail

YIELD: 1 (3-ounce) cocktail

COCKTAIL:
2 ounces rye whiskey
1 ounce sweet vermouth
2 dashes Angostura bitters

Combine rye, vermouth, and bitters in a mixing glass. Add ice and stir. Strain into cocktail glass. Garnish with cherry.

This drink is a universal passkey to pleasure.

The Bellman

BARS AND HOTELS are spaces where hospitality rules the day (and the night). For guests, it's a pleasure, and for the industry's best practitioners, from bellmen to bartenders, it's a craft. Miles Macquarrie gets that. He named his Decatur, Georgia, bar Kimball House, after a grand old Atlanta hotel of the same name. (More on that later in this chapter.)

This well-balanced recipe demands a trip to the bottle shop in the name of continuing cocktail education. Carpano Antica Formula vermouth is a favorite among bartenders for its bitter, spicy, and vanilla notes, and for its viscosity, which lends a rich mouthfeel to drinks. Gran Classico is a bitter aperitivo, made in Switzerland from a nineteenth-century Italian recipe. Think of it as Campari's Alpine border-hopping cousin. Bigallet China-China is an *amer*, the French version of amaro. At 40 percent alcohol by volume, it's on the stronger side for this category. Orange peel is its primary flavor note. The finished drink has a sweet-bitter balance that belies its strength.

GARNISH:
Orange peel

SERVICE ICE:
None

GLASS:
Cocktail

YIELD: 1 (3-ounce) cocktail

COCKTAIL:
1½ ounces rye whiskey
¾ ounce Carpano Antica Formula vermouth
½ ounce Gran Classico
¼ ounce Bigallet China-China *amer* liqueur
4 dashes Angostura bitters

Place ice in the cocktail glass, swirl until glass is chilled, and dump out ice. Combine rye, vermouth, Gran Classico, Bigallet *amer*, and bitters in a mixing glass. Add ice and stir. Strain into chilled cocktail glass and garnish with orange peel.

The Socialist

You always remember your first hit drink, the one that got a call-back after it rotated off the menu. For Atlanta bartender Paul Calvert, this was that drink. Bourbon is not the only dark, barrel-aged, sweet, and beloved Southern spirit, he reminds drinkers. Rum has long been a favorite here, too. Inspired by a Manhattan, benefiting from three types of aged rum, this drink might change your political philosophy.

This recipe doubles as a crash course in rum education, showing you how rum styles vary and how, together, they mesh to form a glorious potable. English-style rum is grassier, with higher notes; Spanish-style is richer, with bottom notes; and Demerara is darker and funkier. Mixed properly, the different levels balance each other.

GARNISH:
Orange twist

SERVICE ICE:
None

GLASS:
Cocktail

YIELD: 1 (3½-ounce) cocktail

COCKTAIL:
¾ ounce Italian vermouth, preferably Carpano Antica Formula
¾ ounce aged English-style rum, such as Scarlet Ibis
¾ ounce aged Spanish-style rum, such as Plantation 5 Year
½ ounce aged Demerara rum, such as Hamilton's
2 dashes orange bitters

Combine vermouth, rums, and bitters in a mixing glass. Add ice and stir until cold. Strain into cocktail glass and garnish with orange twist.

This drink might change your political philosophy.

Bourbon and Gender

ORDERING A DRINK at a bar can be daunting. Maybe you only know of dubious highballs: rum and Coke, Jack and ginger, vodka and Red Bull. What tastes good? What's cool? What's affordable? What will allow you to climb out of bed the next morning? It's enough to keep you muttering "Miller Lite" when the bartender deigns to look your way.

Sooner or later, you mature. You evolve. And so do your tastes in booze. You learn the names of a few cocktails, and you adopt one as your signature. Eventually you order with confidence, and maybe work in a request for a certain liquor or a stylistic preference: "I'll have a dry rye Manhattan." And boom, you've arrived as a grown-up drinker.

If only it were that simple. Ordering a drink in a bar is a performative act. Your preferences, your values, and your very identity are on display in front of your companions, the bartender, and the other patrons.

Perhaps no liquor carries with it more confounding and contradictory implications than whiskey, especially what it says about the gender of the person who orders it. Since its infancy around the turn of the nineteenth century, domestic whiskey distilling has associated itself with the archetypal American man. "Whiskey reflected the strong streak of independence ingrained in the character of the frontier South," Robert Moss writes. And that frontier ideal was inextricably tied to masculinity, valuing physical strength, self-reliance, bravery, and rebellion. "If we need it, we'll make it ourselves" might have been the motto of early rural America. That extended to its first distillers of rye in the Mid-Atlantic states and bourbon in the Appalachian South. Men still buy into this frontier fantasy when they savor a sip of bourbon—even if they left an office job downtown and drove to the bar in a luxury SUV.

Bourbon aficionado and novelist Walker Percy spoke to a similar phenomenon in the 1970s. He wrote of bourbon's power to cut through the ennui that plagued the suburban office worker, husband, and father. He didn't mention the millions of American women who had entered the workforce by the mid-1970s, nor those who stayed at home with the children and might have appreciated a nip of bourbon at the end of a long day. Percy associated drinking bourbon with male socializing, going back to his days as an undergraduate at the University of North Carolina at Chapel Hill. (Before that, he enjoyed bourbon from a Coke bottle passed around the boys' room at high school dances). Often these social occasions involved flirting with or dating women, but it doesn't seem to have mattered much to Percy whether the woman would actually drink the bourbon.

More recently, another UNC graduate explored what drinking bourbon purports to say about one's gender, racial, regional, and class identity. Seán McKeithan's 2012 article "Every Ounce a Man's Whiskey?" turned a 1950s Early Times bourbon advertising slogan into a question, examining what it meant for McKeithan—a young, gay, white Southern man—to drink a liquor that has long been marketed as a symbol of heterosexual white Southern masculinity. Inspired by a college boyfriend's taste for bourbon, McKeithan recalls, "I drank Bourbon in a spirit of transgression that I could not pin down but felt that, in so doing, I took some nebulous stand against the heterosexist assumption that women and queer men drank from glasses that came with umbrellas, instead of only with ice."

While the twenty-first-century bourbon market targets a range of consumers "from the gentleman to the good old boy," McKeithan finds, it still relies on tropes of traditional white Southern masculinity. "In today's South," McKeithan concludes, "Bourbon remains a piece of masculine identity that Southerners can 'put on,' much like overalls, a seersucker suit, or a North Carolina twang."

What happens when women try on the identity that bourbon conveys? Things can get complicated—and, frankly, a little icky—Courtney Balestier writes. "Few drinks have inspired the fetishization of women that whiskey (and its brethren, bourbon and Scotch) has," Balestier argues. "In the pages of men's magazines, where ladies appear with swollen busts and shrunken thighs, the woman who loves whiskey has become such a common trope (seriously, take your pick) that she's already a cliché." Balestier explores this idealized woman, whom she terms a "bro-girl archetype," a sexy badass who drinks like a man while suggesting an unmistakably female—er, prowess. Like her soul sister, the rail-thin-yet-busty dream girl who eats rare cheeseburgers and knows her fantasy football stats, the whiskey woman is a carefully curated persona behind a façade. In all likelihood, she went to a lot of trouble to give the impression that she goes to none at all.

Some of this is changing for the better. Women like Alba Huerta in Houston and Steva Casey in Birmingham are gaining recognition for their work behind the bar. Their drinks aren't known as "girly" or "masculine"—they're recognized as smart, and good. In Kentucky, Marianne Barnes of Castle and Key, a chemical engineer with a learned palate, now works as the Bluegrass State's first female master distiller since Prohibition. She's not even thirty yet.

So what's a drinker of any gender to do when trying to navigate the identity politics of the cocktail list? Order what you damn well please. If you enjoy bourbon, go for it. If you're a burly gentleman with a thirst for vodka and cranberry, you do you. Life is too short to order a drink you don't really love because you're trying to be manly, womanly, cool, or "Southern," whatever that means to you. It's okay if you are the editor of a book about cocktails and you're most likely to reach for a glass of sauvignon blanc. Really, it is. Isn't it? Yes.

SCM

The Bitter Southerner #1

JERRY SLATER concocted this recipe as the first in a series of cocktails commissioned by the *Bitter Southerner* magazine. Overproof bourbon and sorghum yield a mixture that might look like a muddy creek after a heavy rain. Its potency lends "backbone and courage," according to the magazine's editors. Fernet-Branca is a potent amaro made in Milan; its twenty-seven plant-based ingredients coalesce in a strong medicinal flavor. Bartenders love it. Lay drinkers tend to love it or hate it. We say, give it a chance.

GARNISH:
Flamed orange peel

SERVICE ICE:
None

GLASS:
Coupe

YIELD: 1 (3-ounce) cocktail

COCKTAIL:
2 ounces high-proof bourbon, such as Booker's
½ ounce Fernet-Branca
½ ounce sorghum simple syrup (see recipe below)
2 dashes bourbon-barrel-aged bitters, such as Fee's

Combine bourbon, Fernet-Branca, sorghum syrup, and bitters in a mixing glass. Add ice and stir. Strain into coupe. Cut a 1-inch round piece of peel from the orange. Flame the peel (see under Techniques, page 170) and add to the drink.

SORGHUM SIMPLE SYRUP
¼ cup boiling water
¼ cup sorghum syrup

Combine water and sorghum in a small heatproof bowl or container and stir until sorghum dissolves. Refrigerate in an airtight container for up to 1 month.
Yield: ½ cup

The Prestidigitator

HAT TRICK GIN is the flagship spirit of High Wire Distilling in Charleston. Some gin drinkers are creatures of habit—*don't mess with my tonic, thankyouverymuch*. But for those who like to mix things up, High Wire also offers Hat Trick in a six-month barrel-rested version. The magician depicted on the bottle inspired this loose interpretation of a Martinez, a nineteenth-century cocktail of Old Tom gin, sweet vermouth, bitters, and maraschino liqueur. Here the Madeira serves as a nod to High Wire's hometown, where that fortified wine was the colonial-era drink of choice among the elite.

GARNISH:
Brandied cherry

SERVICE ICE:
None

GLASS:
Martini

YIELD: 1 (3½-ounce) cocktail

COCKTAIL:
1½ ounces barrel-rested gin, such as High Wire Hat Trick
1 ounce sweet vermouth, such as Cocchi di Torino
½ ounce Madeira, such as Broadbent Rainwater
2 dashes orange bitters

Combine gin, vermouth, Madeira, and bitters in a mixing glass. Add ice and stir. Strain into martini glass and garnish with cherry.

Fightin' Words

BIRMINGHAM-BASED Eric Bennett calls this drink a Manhattan cousin that's a little rough around the edges—in the best way. It shows an excellent balance of herbal, bitter, and just a touch of sweet.

GARNISH:
Orange peel

SERVICE ICE:
None

GLASS:
Rocks

YIELD: 1 (3¼-ounce) cocktail

COCKTAIL:
2 ounces rye
¾ ounce Cocchi Americano Rosa
¼ ounce Fernet-Branca
¼ ounce simple syrup (see recipe page 174)
1 dash Angostura bitters
3 drops orange blossom water

Stir ingredients with ice in a mixing glass. Strain into a rocks glass and garnish with a flamed orange peel (see under Techniques, page 170).

Kimball House

THIS DRINK—and the Decatur, Georgia, bar of which it is the house cocktail—takes its name from a grand hotel in downtown Atlanta built in 1870 and demolished in 1959. A version of a classic Martini, it conjures an era of elegance. If you've always beenintimidated by Martinis, start here, and sip slowly.

Kimball House offers a sort of choose-your-own-garnish adventure, serving the drink with a small pewter bowl containing a segment of lemon peel and two unstuffed, house-brined cocktail olives. When you mix this drink at home, go with your garnish of choice, or treat yourself to both. (If you twist the lemon peel into the drink and nibble on the olives as a snack, we won't tell.)

GARNISH:
Lemon peel and/or
cocktail olives

SERVICE ICE:
None

GLASS:
Cocktail

YIELD: 1 (3½-ounce) cocktail

COCKTAIL:
2 ounces London dry gin
½ ounce dry vermouth, such as Dolin dry
½ ounce Cocchi Americano
2 dashes orange bitters
Green Chartreuse (optional)*

Combine gin, vermouth, Cocchi Americano, and bitters in a mixing glass. Add ice and stir for 15 seconds. Strain into cocktail glass, squeeze lemon peel over the surface of the drink, and discard.

*This is how they serve it at Kimball House: Using an eyedropper, drop 10 drops green Chartreuse onto the surface and enjoy.

Edgewood

In the great tradition of naming cocktails after beloved neighborhoods (think Manhattan or Red Hook) comes a complex sour named for a community on the east side of Atlanta. Greg Best chose Edgewood as his home when he first moved to Atlanta. In those years he began taking craft cocktails seriously—he chose to get lost in the woods rather than stand at the edge.

Speaking of new experiences, if you've never tried it, think of Cynar as a sort of gateway amaro. It's easier to find than many of its brethren, and it plays nicely in cocktails, or by itself with club soda and an orange twist. Don't let the artichoke scare you off. The flavor is less thorny than you might think.

GARNISH:
Pinch of sea salt

SERVICE ICE:
None

GLASS:
Cocktail

YIELD: 1 (3-ounce) cocktail

COCKTAIL:
1 ounce London dry gin
1 ounce freshly squeezed white grapefruit juice
½ ounce Portuguese muscat wine
½ ounce artichoke liqueur, such as Cynar

Place crushed ice in a cocktail glass, swirl to chill, dump out ice, and set glass aside. Combine gin, grapefruit juice, wine, and artichoke liqueur in a shaker. Add ice and shake. Double-strain into the chilled glass and garnish with a pinch of salt.

McKinney's Pond

As a child, Hunt Revell loved to eat at McKinney's Pond, a country-style restaurant in rural Midville, Georgia. He remembers the fried gator, the frog's legs, the steaks, the oysters, the on-site skating rink, and the owner, whose name was Muck. At the time, Revell was too young to partake of the buckets of lite beer that the adults enjoyed. He is now the bartender at Seabear Oyster Bar in Athens, Georgia, where he created this loose Manhattan riff as an homage to McKinney's Pond. Kronan Swedish Punsch, a sugarcane-based liqueur reminiscent of a low-proof rum with sweet and spicy notes, takes the place of sweet vermouth.

GARNISH:
Lime twist

SERVICE ICE:
Single large
cube

GLASS:
Rocks

YIELD: 1 (3-ounce) cocktail

COCKTAIL:
1 ounce bourbon, such as Belle Meade Sour Mash
1 ounce Jamaican rum, such as Hamilton Jamaican Pot Still Gold
1 ounce Kronan Swedish Punsch
3 dashes lime bitters, such as Scrappy's

Stir ingredients with some ice in a mixing glass. Strain into a rocks glass with large ice cube and garnish with a lime twist.

McKinney's Pond was a country-style restaurant in rural Midville, Georgia.

7

Spirits, Enhanced
Old-Fashioned

Make an Old-Fashioned and You Have Transformed Whiskey

"What's your favorite cocktail?" "What do you drink at home?"

I'm asked those questions a lot. I founded an Atlanta bar and restaurant that earned a bit of a reputation for elaborate cocktails and a well-stocked whiskey selection. After I teach a cocktail or bourbon class, patrons frequently ask about my own drinking habits. I sometimes worry about disappointing the enthusiasts with my simple answer: I drink Old-Fashioneds. Okay, I also drink Manhattans, and various improvisations on Manhattans. I drink a lot of wine with my sommelier wife, and I occasionally just want a cold beer after a long day. But my answer is ready when someone asks, "What is your cocktail of choice?" The Old-Fashioned is it.

Like the majority of chefs I know, who don't cook elaborately at home, off-duty I keep it simple. My work space is better stocked for pomp and circumstance. At home, a bottle of bourbon, a bottle of bitters, and some cubes of sugar are enough. If I remembered to fill the ice tray that makes large cubes, or to steal a lemon from work, things are better. But neither is necessary.

An Old-Fashioned made in the old-fashioned way is the drink equivalent of rustic Italian cuisine: simple and elegant. Take a sugar cube (I prefer brown for its kiss of molasses, but white will do), add a couple of dashes of Angostura bitters, and muddle with a half-ounce of water. Add two ounces of bourbon—rye is just fine, too—and a large cube of ice or two. Stir, and garnish with a spritz of citrus oil from a long strip of lemon peel.

This may not be the Old-Fashioned that you grew up with. There is another "Old-Fashioned" out there that involves pulverizing an orange and a candied cherry with a packet of sugar. A purveyor of such drinks sometimes adds bitters. Sometimes he forgets. After, he adds a little whiskey and a lot of ice. If this wasn't enough to make you order a beer, that bartender finishes the murky, fruity drink with a generous splash of soda water, insulting your whiskey and throwing said cocktail further out of balance. There is a theory that this "Old-Fashioned" came to prominence during Prohibition, when bad whiskey needed to be masked. I believe it.

Others say the Old-Fashioned was created at the Pendennis Club in Louisville. As the story goes, it was first mixed by, or for, a bourbon distiller by the name of Colonel James E. Pepper around the turn of the twentieth century. This is such a pervasive story that I repeated it at a Southern Foodways Alliance summer field trip in 2008. That afternoon Julian Van Winkle III made Old-Fashioneds for everyone in the famed club's pool room, giving further credence to the tale.

Dave Wondrich points out that the original "cock tail" dates back to 1806 and includes spirits, bitters, water, and sugar. A hundred years later, to have a cocktail in the old-fashioned style was as much an adjective as it was a noun. Bartenders never like to let the truth get in the way of a good story. As a turn-of-the-century bourbon distiller, Colonel Pepper didn't let truth stop him from using the story to hawk his wares at the Waldorf-Astoria in New York City, where Old-Fashioneds became popular.

Make an Old-Fashioned and you have transformed whiskey. A potent and singular spirit has been bittered, sweetened, mellowed, chilled, and bequeathed a bright note of lemon. The drink evolves as you sip it. It starts off strong and bracing, as the spice of the bitters marries the whiskey's sweeter tones. In a proper glass, the drink has weight, and the clink of large ice cubes against its sides tolls a welcome tune. Give your glass a slight shake to hear it.

As the ice melts slowly, an Old-Fashioned becomes easier and easier to drink, until, about three-quarters of the way through, it might become too sweet. Now is the time for a patch. Just one more ounce, maybe one more ice cube, to put the drink, and therefore the world, back in balance.

JS

Old-Fashioned

GARNISH:
Lemon peel

SERVICE ICE:
Cubed

GLASS:
Rocks

YIELD: 1 (2½-ounce) cocktail

COCKTAIL:
1 Demerara sugar cube
3 dashes Angostura bitters
½ ounce water
2 ounces bourbon

Place sugar cube, bitters, and water in a rocks glass. Muddle to dissolve. Add bourbon and ice and stir. Squeeze lemon peel over drink and place peel in glass.

Sherried Old-Fashioned

THIS RECIPE forgoes sugar in favor of another Southern colonial favorite, sherry. Try a Pedro Ximénez (the name refers to the grape), which is rich, nutty, and slightly bitter. Derek Brown, proprietor of Mockingbird Hill in Washington, D.C., created this cocktail to give whiskey drinkers something to enjoy at a sherry bar.

GARNISH:
Orange peel

SERVICE ICE:
Cubed

GLASS:
Double rocks

YIELD: 1 (2¼-ounce) cocktail

COCKTAIL:
2 ounces bourbon
¼ ounce sherry, such as Pedro Ximénez
1 dash Angostura bitters

Combine bourbon, sherry, and bitters in a mixing glass. Add ice and stir. Strain into ice-filled double rocks glass and garnish with orange peel.

[Pop]Corn from a Jar

MARVIN "POPCORN" SUTTON, at the wheel of his Model A Ford, bumps along a gravel road in the Smoky Mountains until he spies the perfect streamside site. Using mud and rocks, solder and wheat paste, a copper pot and a galvanized metal trash can, he constructs a still. It's a jerry-rigged beauty, the type of contraption you'd see in old photos surrounded by the fedora-wearing lawmen who would soon bust it to pieces.

This particular still, though also illegal, was to be operated under a higher cultural license. Sutton, with help from his friend J. B. Rader, built it for the North Carolina filmmaker Neal Hutcheson, who edited his footage into a film called *The Last One*. That documentary, broadcast on PBS stations, earned Hutcheson an Emmy and turned Popcorn Sutton into a celebrity moonshiner, the man who preserved the ancient mountain tradition of squeezing liquor out of corn.

Sutton's work reflected some modern influences. Late in the film, when the still springs a leak, Sutton patches it with a dab of wheat paste and a strip of cloth torn from a clean white undershirt. ("That paste—when the heat hits it, it gets harder than a minister's dick," he says.)

"Believe it or not," Sutton explains as he ties the cloth around a pipe, "I learned this trick right here off that Snuffy Smith shit in the newspaper." The authentic Appalachian moonshiner, in other words, had learned his trade, in part, from a comic-strip hillbilly.

Snuffy Smith—poker cheat, chicken thief, moonshiner—sprang from the mind of Billy DeBeck, who studied at the Chicago Academy of Fine Arts before he took up cartooning. DeBeck first hit it big in the 1920s with *Barney Google*, a strip about a top-hatted lover of horse races and prizefights. In a 1934 storyline, Barney Google paid a visit to the fictional North Carolina mountain hamlet of Hootin' Holler, where he met Snuffy Smith, who proved so popular with readers that he became the strip's star.

It was the heyday of the hillbilly. The Al Capp comic *Li'l Abner*, set in the Kentucky mountains, also began during the Great Depression. Together the two strips cemented the stereotype in the American mind. Pop culture depictions would range from gentle (*The Beverly Hillbillies*) to vicious (*Deliverance*) but always portray Appalachia as a region bypassed by civilization. Actual residents of the mountains, already struggling with poverty and economic exploitation, now faced the condescension of outsiders who confused cartoons with reality.

A few mountain folk saw a way to turn stereotypes to their advantage, especially as the region's economy shifted toward tourism. The hillbilly took up residence on signs advertising the gift shops and hotels of the Smokies, beckoning tourists with the promise of an imagined Appalachia.

Popcorn Sutton took the marketing a step further. He was the real thing. A native of Haywood County, North Carolina, Sutton learned bootlegging from his grandfather and was known to distill a high-quality liquor. By the time he became an adult, however, commercial liquor was legal and cheap, and the true outlaws of Appalachia trafficked in methamphetamine and marijuana.

The mood-altering substance Popcorn peddled was not so much ethanol as ersatz nostalgia. Some friends of his owned a bed-and-breakfast in Maggie Valley. Sutton parked his Model A in the yard and contributed artifacts to help decorate the Moonshiner Suite. Notoriety, Sutton knew, increased demand for his product, which at times brought $100 a gallon. If tourists wanted to buy moonshine from a hillbilly, he'd sell it to them at a premium.

Popcorn Sutton played the role of an X-rated Snuffy Smith. Like the cartoon character, Sutton was a tiny man who wore overalls and misshapen hats. Sutton's hat, however, had a raccoon's penis bone tucked into the band, and his sense of humor was not fit for the newspaper. In an interview with Johnny Knoxville of *Jackass* fame, Sutton detailed his preference for plus-sized women and showed off the mirrors on his bedroom ceiling. He also displayed a granite grave marker he'd commissioned: Future visitors to his final resting place would be greeted with the message POPCORN SAID FUCK YOU.

A friend once warned him, "You can't be a movie star and make liquor, too."

"You can't sell it if no one knows you have it," Sutton replied.

They were both right. In 2008 federal agents raided his property in Cocke County, Tennessee, and discovered hundreds of gallons of moonshine and a 1,000-gallon, gas-fired, stainless-steel still in which Sutton cooked a mash from sugar, not corn. That copper pot in the woods was strictly for marketing.

Sutton pleaded guilty and asked the judge for leniency, explaining that he suffered from chronic obstructive pulmonary disorder and might not survive a stint in prison. He was sentenced to eighteen months. Just before he was due to report to prison, Sutton committed suicide by running a hose from the tailpipe through the window of his Ford Fairlane. He was sixty-two. His wife, Pam Sutton, explained that her husband called the Fairlane his "three-gallon car" because he'd acquired it in trade for that much whiskey.

His name lives on at Popcorn Sutton Distilling, makers of Popcorn Sutton's Tennessee White Whiskey (bottled at a modest 88 proof). Pam Sutton is a partner in the Newport, Tennessee–based business, which revealed its lofty ambitions in 2015 when it hired away George Dickel's master distiller. The firm uses neither the ramshackle still Sutton built in the woods nor the stainless-steel behemoth he fired up for his production runs, but gleaming copper-pot stills that would look at home in any craft distillery.

It's hard to imagine Sutton's former customers finding what they were looking for amid all that high-end equipment. Sutton sold more than white whiskey, just as Snuffy Smith offered something beyond mockery of mountain folk. Snuffy may have been a "shif'less skonk," but shiftlessness offers liberation from respectable society and its tedious demand to hold steady jobs and obey the law. Generations of newspaper readers, scanning the funny papers over coffee before shuffling off to work, must have felt a twinge of admiration as Snuffy outwitted Sheriff Tait and then took a nap in the woods. Popcorn Sutton brought that criminality to life and gave it an uncomfortably jagged edge.

According to the website of Popcorn Sutton Distilling, "the only difference between our 'likker' and Popcorn's is that we pay our taxes." But that difference is everything. With moonshine, the illicit is the appeal. That burn in the throat tastes like freedom.

ME

Rum Old-Fashioned

THIS IS AN IMPROVISATION, a cocktail made in the "old-fashioned way" with the South's original brown liquor. Choose a rich, aged, but not overly sweet rum. Orange bitters and two types of citrus brighten the unctuous traits. Many bars will make you a rum Old-Fashioned. Try one at Cane and Table in New Orleans, where rum rules the menu.

GARNISH:
Orange and
lemon peel

SERVICE ICE:
Cubed

GLASS:
Rocks

YIELD: 1 (2½-ounce) cocktail

COCKTAIL:
1 Demerara sugar cube
2 dashes orange bitters
2 dashes Angostura bitters
½ ounce water
2 ounces aged rum

Place sugar cube, both bitters, and water in a rocks glass. Muddle to dissolve. Add rum and ice and stir. Squeeze orange and lemon peels over drink and place peels in glass.

An Old-Fashioned made in the old-fashioned way is simple and elegant.

Añejo Old-Fashioned

IN 2007 the New York bartender Phillip Ward, then at Death & Company, stirred a national hit with his Oaxaca Old-Fashioned. This is a take on that recipe, designed to appeal to bourbon and tequila fans alike. Tequila and its smoky cousin mezcal are on the rise these days. If you're still under the mistaken impression that tequila is the province of overserved spring breakers, begin your appreciation for its grown-up potential with this recipe.

GARNISH:
Grapefruit peel

YIELD: 1 (2½-ounce) cocktail

COCKTAIL:
1 Demerara sugar cube

SERVICE ICE:
Cubed

2 dashes grapefruit bitters

1 dash Angostura bitters

GLASS:
Rocks

½ ounce water

2 ounces añejo tequila, such as Fortaleza

Place sugar cube, both bitters, and water in a rocks glass. Muddle to dissolve. Add tequila and ice and stir. Squeeze grapefruit peel over drink and place peel in glass.

The Unvanquished

NAMED AFTER THE William Faulkner novel, this bourbon cocktail benefits from an intriguing mix of sharp and resiny aromas and tastes. Zirbenz, a pine liqueur, might not be a Yoknapatawpha County product, but it does remind us of the sentinel pines of Mississippi. Trust us—this drink will have you puffing out your chest like Colonel Sartoris.

GARNISH:
None

SERVICE ICE:
Single large cube

GLASS:
Rocks

YIELD: 1 (3-ounce) cocktail

COCKTAIL:
3 cardamom pods
1½ ounces bourbon
½ ounce Zirbenz
½ ounce maple syrup
½ ounce freshly squeezed lime juice
1 dash orange bitters

Muddle cardamom pods in a cocktail shaker. Add remaining ingredients and some ice and shake. Double-strain into glass with large ice cube.

Keepers of Chipped Dreams

I CALL HIM EZEKIEL, that 1969 Cabin Still ceramic bourbon decanter on my work desk molded in the shape of a stereotypical hillbilly. Bearded, barefoot, and slouching on a barrel, wearing a floppy hat and overalls and holding a shotgun and a whiskey jug, he looks like Ezekiel. That is to say, he's a dead ringer for my favorite uncle, *mi tío* Ezequiel.

Ezekiel the Decanter has guarded my office since 2013. I bought him somewhere in Kentucky as part of my pickings from the 127 Yard Sale, that mega-flea-market happening held the first weekend of every August, spanning from Gadsden, Alabama, through Covington, Kentucky. I'll always keep Ezekiel close to me, not because it cost $25 to score him and a two-foot-tall companion statue, but because that's the summer I decided to collect as many bourbon decanters as possible.

Decanters had intrigued me ever since I saw a 1997 *Simpsons* episode where Marge told a novelty store owner (voiced by cult director John Waters) that a Confederate soldier statue owned by her grandmother was worth a fortune. The store owner pointed out that it was just a whiskey holder that cost "two books of green stamps, if I'm not mistaken."

My eighteen-year-old self laughed doubly—at the joke, yes, and at the idea that anyone would ever want to collect such cheesy things. Commemorative china plates, I understood. Porcelain dolls, sure. But bourbon decanters molded in the shape of humans? How déclassé. How antiquated.

Today I own more than forty of them, in the form of: The state of Ohio. A train. The legendary thoroughbred Man o' War. Old cannons. King Kamehameha. The Governor's Palace in Williamsburg, Virginia. Special editions honoring the 200th anniversary of California's Catholic mission system, and celebrating the Rocky Mountains. Do I have a bottle citing the third running of the Kentucky Pacing Derby at the old Louisville Downs? You know it!

What changed? Well, I'm older now. Collecting ceramic bourbon decanters (also known as figurals) is a cheaper and more age-appropriate hobby than model trains. It helps that I'm a functioning *borracho* fascinated by bourbon culture. I used to think of these bottles as a punchline. Now I see them for what they are: keepers of chipped dreams.

They were a national obsession for decades for the Silent Majority, a buttress against Flower Power's chaos and the materialism of the Me Decade. People bought, sold, and traded them with the same vigor once devoted to swapping baseball cards or Beanie Babies. Clubs formed around the passion. Newspapers heralded conventions where hobbyists brought their wares for an impressed public to view. Collecting bourbon decanters was a way for working-class folks to feel like they were investing in something tangible that could double as decoration.

When I buy figural decanters during the 127 Yard Sale, the vendors always package them carefully, whether they're in mint condition or have faded colors or labels. It's bittersweet for them. They just made a sale, but many start telling me stories about the decanter while searching for newspaper and bubble wrap: how long it was in their family, the fun the bourbon inspired.

IN THE 1940s, Jim Beam began issuing fancy bottles under its Pin Bottle series, so named because they were molded in the shape of bowling pins. In 1955, for the 160th anniversary of the brand, Beam unveiled a Royal Porcelain Anniversary Bottle, containing hooch aged 160 months. "Beam Bottles were never meant to be concealed," boasted a 1955 *Life* holiday ad for the collectible. It featured a man in suit and tie sitting at a table with his hands behind his back, happily gazing at the Royal Porcelain and Pin Bottle before him as other presents remained wrapped, already forgotten. An industry was born.

Jim Beam released multiple bottles each year, and competitors followed suit. The bourbon decanter fad didn't become an American phenomenon until Mike Wayne, the visionary vice president of Ezra Brooks, came on the scene. Wayne was a bourbon veteran. He joined the industry in 1933 and helped Ezra Brooks enter the figural game in 1967 with a replica flintlock. In 1969 Wayne issued a decanter in the shape of the eighteen-karat Golden Rooster on display at the Nugget Casino in Sparks, Nevada. Originally priced at $15, it went for more than $200 within months.

As the trend took off, Jim Beam and Ezra Brooks invested in factories to mass-produce decanters, creating a china race. Regardless of producer, decanter subjects were gloriously square even by 1970s standards. Popular themes included wildlife, famous buildings, homages to states and pioneer days. Wild Turkey featured its namesake bird. Beam and Brooks offered limited-edition bottles to commemorate conventions, liquor stores, college football bowl games, and fraternal organizations.

THE DECANTER'S GLORY DAYS arguably ended in the summer of 1987, when the McCormick Distilling Company announced they were releasing their thirty-seventh and final Elvis Presley figural. "We feel we've done our thing with Elvis. He's been good to us," a vice president told the AP. After more than 120,000 sold, ranging in price from $65 to $400, the firm was moving on. And so was nearly everyone else.

I find it telling that, in the present day, the one spirit that carries on the tradition of chintzy bottling is tequila. From bottles shaped like skulls to guns, agave plants, big-breasted women, classy pottery, Aztec emperors, and more, many a middle-class Mexican American home proudly shows off its collection, long after the tequila is gone. Like a previous generation of Americans with their bourbon figurals, a tequila decanter for Mexican Americans is not just a decanter. It's a signifier of culture, a marker of aspirations, a keeper of ambition.

GA

Canebrake Cooler

WHEN DAVID WONDRICH looks into his crystal ball, he sees a hotter, wetter South in which sugarcane will thrive. He imagines the juice becoming a mainstay in restaurants, where it will add a grassy sweetness to beverages from iced tea to rum to whiskey. This drink is built on a base of corn whiskey and is often aged in previously used oak barrels. The result is a softer-tasting, grainier spirit that won't overwhelm a subtle flavor like cane juice. Dash some bitters on top, and you have a simple cocktail that's refreshing, spicy, and delicious.

GARNISH:
Lime wedge, optional

SERVICE ICE:
Cubed

GLASS:
Highball

YIELD: 1 (5-ounce) cocktail

COCKTAIL:

2 ounces bonded corn whiskey, such as Mellow Corn

3 ounces sugarcane juice (freshly pressed is ideal but can be hard to come by; Goya makes a canned version)

2 to 3 dashes bitters, Angostura or your choice

Combine corn whiskey and sugarcane juice in an ice-filled highball glass. Dash bitters on top to your liking. Stir and serve with a straw and a lime wedge, if desired.

This drink is built on a base of corn whiskey.

7th Ward

BEFORE MATT MCFERRON opened the Old Pal in Athens, Georgia, he lived in New Orleans. The Crescent City has inspired many of his cocktail creations, in the form of ingredients, drink names, or, in this case, both. You could make this drink with another spiced rum, but it's worth seeking out Old New Orleans Cajun Spice, distilled from Louisiana sugarcane and blended with allspice and nutmeg. Rich syrup is made from a 1:2 ratio of water to sugar. Here it balances the spice of the rum and the bite of the Fernet, but simple syrup (1:1) is an acceptable substitute.

GARNISH:
Grapefruit peel

SERVICE ICE:
None

GLASS:
Rocks

YIELD: 1 (3-ounce) cocktail

COCKTAIL:
1½ ounces spiced rum, such as Old New Orleans Cajun Spice
½ ounce Fernet-Branca
½ ounce rich syrup, or substitute simple syrup (see recipe page 174)
½ ounce freshly squeezed grapefruit juice
2 dashes Angostura bitters

Combine ingredients with ice in a shaker. Shake and strain into rocks glass. Garnish with a grapefruit peel.

8

Potent Prescriptions
Sazerac

Rye Not?

Remember how, in the Brandy Milk Punch chapter, we talked about New Orleans's historic predilection for brandy? And how, in the Mint Julep chapter, we explained that brandy, not bourbon, was the drink's original base? Add the Sazerac to the list of iconic cocktails whose main ingredient shifted from brandy to domestic brown liquor in the second half of the nineteenth century.

Sazerac brand cognac was popular in New Orleans into the mid-1800s. It became the name of a coffeehouse. Back then, the Sazerac coffeehouse sold as many cocktails as cups of coffee. In the 1850s a pharmacist named Antoine Amédée Peychaud started selling herbal concoctions steeped in alcohol and marketing them as health aids. Along with an absinthe rinse, a hint of sugar, and a lemon peel, these bitters were the base ingredient for the original Sazerac.

That became the signature drink of the Sazerac coffeehouse. The drink itself might not have gone by that name right away. "Sazerac is a style of drink that then earned a name," explains bartender Chris Hannah, citing colleague Chris McMillian. "Everybody was rinsing their spirits with absinthe and medicinal bitters back then," Hannah says. "And then just because the Sazerac House became famous, they named their house drink, which is what everybody was drinking, the Sazerac."

Hannah and McMillian are probably right. It wasn't until about 1900 that a drink known as the Sazerac gained popularity beyond New Orleans. Between 1900 and 1910, newspapers from Atlanta to Chicago to Washington, D.C., sang its praises. By then the standard recipe called for rye. But there was still room for improvisation. "The Sazerac is consistently the most inconsistently made cocktail in the history of cocktails," says Hannah. He's not just talking about the shift from cognac to rye. Once absinthe distilling was outlawed in the United States, Herbsaint became the standard for rinsing the Sazerac glass. Bartenders may even substitute another anise-flavored spirit, such as pastis. As for the bitters, Peychaud's are nonnegotiable, though some Sazerac recipes call for a dose of Angostura as well. And then there's the question of the lemon peel. Should you express and discard, or leave it in the glass?

Here's where we stand: If you want to be true to the drink's New Orleans roots, choose Herbsaint over French absinthe for rinsing. Pour a little in a rocks glass, roll it to coat the sides of the glass, and pour out the excess. Some New Orleans bartenders give the glass a little twist-and-toss move. Practice this a few times before you adopt it as your own party trick. To the Sazerac rye, add simple syrup (it's easier than muddling a sugar cube) and Peychaud's bitters for color, aroma, and flavor. The bright red bitters lend the Sazerac its signature pinkish cast. After stirring the drink in a mixing glass and straining it into the rinsed rocks glass (ice in the mixing glass, yes; ice in the serving glass, no), express the lemon peel and drop it into the glass. If you've never ordered a Sazerac before, the finished product can look almost dinky—three measly ounces of liquid and no ice? You might be tempted to knock it back too quickly. We advise moderation. As you learn the ways of the Sazerac, you'll learn to appreciate measured sips.

The Metairie, Louisiana–based Sazerac company now manages an extensive portfolio of liquor brands, including Sazerac rye, Herbsaint, and Peychaud's bitters. It's almost as if the company vertically integrated and consolidated its namesake cocktail.

Down the road from Metairie in New Orleans proper, local bartenders cite the Sazerac as a drink that never disappeared from the New Orleans barscape, even when other old-school cocktails fell out of favor. "I make so many Sazeracs that I can make them in my sleep," Bobby Oakes, Chris Hannah's predecessor at Arnaud's French 75 Bar, told SFA oral historian Amy Evans in 2005. At that early point in the craft cocktail revival, few if any bartenders outside New Orleans could say the same. Before the restaurant finally built a bar in 1997, waiters at Galatoire's mixed Sazeracs at the host stand for decades. The ability to make a Sazerac was, and is, a necessary skill for the New Orleans professional.

These days, you don't have to travel to New Orleans to get a proper Sazerac. Crook's Corner in North Carolina stirs a reliable version. At that black-and-white tiled bar, a Chapel Hill landmark, one sip is enough to transport you 800-plus miles to the Crescent City.

SCM

Sazerac

GARNISH:	YIELD: 1 (2½-ounce) cocktail
Lemon peel	
	COCKTAIL:
SERVICE ICE:	2 ounces rye whiskey
None	½ ounce simple syrup (see recipe page 174)
	4 dashes Peychaud's bitters
GLASS:	Absinthe for rinsing, preferably Herbsaint 100*
Rocks	

Place rye, simple syrup, and bitters in a mixing glass. Add ice and stir. Rinse a chilled rocks glass with absinthe. Strain cocktail into rinsed glass, squeeze lemon peel over drink, and place peel in glass.

*There are two versions of Herbsaint: 90 proof and 100 proof "original." The "original" is a reproduction of a 1934 recipe. Even though it is higher proof, it has a milder and more herbaceous anise flavor. And the retro label is dope.

Sazerac brand cognac was popular in New Orleans into the mid-1800s.

Sazerac Sour

THIS COCKTAIL TAKES the Sazerac to a new level. First you create a Sazerac-flavored syrup. Then you add that to the traditional elements of a Sazerac and shake it into a refreshing sour with a beautiful, deep watermelon color. If a regular Sazerac is too elemental for you, give this one a try.

GARNISH:
Lemon peel

SERVICE ICE:
None

GLASS:
Rocks

YIELD: 1 (3½-ounce) cocktail

COCKTAIL:
1½ ounces rye whiskey
½ ounce freshly squeezed lemon juice
½ ounce Sazerac syrup (see recipe below)
½ ounce Peychaud's bitters
4 dashes Angostura bitters
¼ ounce Herbsaint

Place ice in a rocks glass, swirl until chilled, dump out ice, and set glass aside. Combine rye, lemon juice, Sazerac syrup, bitters, and Herbsaint in a cocktail shaker. Add ice and shake. Strain into the chilled glass and garnish with lemon peel.

SAZERAC SYRUP
½ cup honey
¼ cup water
¾ cup sugar
½ cup rye whiskey
1 ounce Peychaud's bitters
½ ounce Angostura bitters
4 one-inch-long pieces lemon peel

Place all ingredients in a small saucepan, set over high heat, and bring to a boil. Decrease heat to low and simmer for 5 minutes. Remove lemon peel and refrigerate syrup in an airtight glass container for up to 1 month.
Yield: Approximately 2 cups

Louisville to New Orleans

ONE IS THE Mint Julep capital and the home of the Seelbach. The other is the cradle of the Sazerac, the Ramos Gin Fizz, and the Vieux Carré. River cities with rich histories of commerce, Louisville and New Orleans are the twin poles of Southern cocktail culture. Their kinship stretches back more than two hundred years.

Jean-Baptiste Le Moyne de Bienville founded New Orleans as the capital of French Louisiana in 1718, on a curve in the Mississippi River. Sixty years later a Virginian-born military officer named George Rogers Clark set up camp at what would become Louisville, Kentucky, at the Falls of the Ohio River, accompanied by a crew of soldiers and a few score civilian settlers. From a frontier base in Louisville, a nascent United States would defend itself against British and Native American threats.

At the close of the Revolutionary War, farmers and merchants west of the Appalachian Mountains were searching for efficient ways to transport their goods to market. The trip across the mountains to major East Coast cities like New York, Philadelphia, and Baltimore was shorter, but cargo was slow, expensive, and dangerous to transport. It may seem counterintuitive when looking at a map, but at the turn of the nineteenth century, the most efficient solution for merchants in Ohio and Mississippi River cities was to load a barge with corn, wheat, hogs, or, yes, whiskey, and float it downriver to New Orleans. From the 1780s until 1802, the Spanish controlled the Mississippi River south of Vicksburg, blocking American access to the port of New Orleans and frustrating entrepreneurs upriver in cities like Louisville. The Louisiana Purchase of 1803 opened up the river all the way to the Gulf of Mexico, and commerce boomed.*

From the port of New Orleans, the goods could be sold locally, exported abroad, or shipped around Florida and north to one of the East Coast ports. Getting the goods down to New Orleans was the easy part. Bringing the barge, crew, and return cargo back north was another story. Some shipping companies broke down the empty flatboats and sold them for lumber, leaving the crew to make the return trip on land. Otherwise, the trip to Louisville or Memphis or St. Louis was just as much of a pain in the rear as you might imagine. Crews managed with tedious methods that depended on the weather and the river's depth and width. These techniques included pushing off the bottom with wooden poles to propel the boat against the current, or trudging along the banks pulling ropes tied to the barge, literally tugging the flatboat along.

Let's pause for a moment and consider the state of domestic distilling circa 1800. We already know that rum and brandy were the East Coast spirits of choice in the colonial era. In addition to the imported stuff from the Caribbean (rum) and France (brandy), enterprising home distillers crafted brandy from apples and, in the Carolina and Georgia colonies, peaches. Domestic whiskey came a little later, first in the form of rye from Pennsylvania, New York, and western Maryland, then corn whiskey from Kentucky, which came to be called bourbon after one of the commonwealth's original counties. (When Kentucky became a state in 1792, Bourbon County covered much more territory than it does today.) By about 1800, a taste and a market developed for these spirits beyond their places of origin.

In his book *The Alcoholic Republic*, W. J. Rorabaugh offers an impressive array of statistics on the whiskey-making success of early distillers and the drinking habits of early Americans. He helpfully tallies the flow of whiskey down the Ohio and Mississippi Rivers. "In 1812, New Orleans received 11,000 gallons of whiskey," Rorabaugh reports. Because the river was the I-55 of its day, virtually all of this whiskey would have arrived by boat. Just twelve years later, in 1824, 570,000 gallons of whiskey were hauled ashore in the Crescent City. Let's take an even heftier statistic from Louisville during the same period. In 1810, 250,000 gallons of whiskey traveled past the Falls of the Ohio. That figure would have included Kentucky bourbon as well as Monongahela rye that probably originated at Pittsburgh. By 1822, more than two *million* gallons floated past the falls. A single invention made this possible: the steamship.

The first steamship navigated the Ohio and Mississippi Rivers in the winter of 1811–12. In the years that followed, the trip between Louisville and New Orleans became faster in both directions. Three and a half years after that first trip, it took less than a month for a steamship to return to Louisville from New Orleans. By 1850 it was a week. Steamship cargo and passenger transit on the Ohio and Mississippi Rivers peaked in the 1830s and continued to thrive until around the 1850s, when the railroad usurped the river's traffic.

In the days of barges, a merchant might send goods to market in New Orleans just once a year. As those whiskey statistics make clear, steamships' speed and their ability to travel upriver as well as down multiplied the volume and frequency of river trade. Today Kentucky bourbon distillers love to tell the story of how bourbon, aged on the voyage from Louisville to New Orleans, arrived in the Crescent City smoother and richer than when it left the Bluegrass State. While their take on the effects of waterborne aging is likely heavy on romance and marketing, there might be a little truth to it, too.

New Orleans's population boomed in the half century between the Louisiana Purchase and the Civil War. Census data suggests that it was the fastest-growing city in the United States between 1830 and 1840. By the early 1850s it was the nation's fifth-largest city. In addition to the swell in its permanent population, New Orleans also welcomed tens of thousands of visitors. They arrived thirsty. In *Southern Spirits*, Robert Moss argues that the business climate lubricated New Orleans. It's certainly plausible: Deals have long been closed over a round of drinks. It's fun to think of 1830s river merchants as Creole Mad Men.

That commerce-leads-to-cocktails logic works in Louisville, too. In both nineteenth-century cities, hotels were centers of cocktail culture for the merchant classes. In the mid-1800s, grand hotels with elegant, well-stocked bars rose along the river, including the Louisville Hotel and the Galt House in Louisville and the Hotel Royal and the St. Charles Hotel in New Orleans. In Louisville, a gentleman could order a whiskey cocktail—a close ancestor of today's Old-Fashioned—or, yes, a Mint Julep. (Before you get too romantic, remember that the Derby-julep affiliation, and by extension the Louisville-julep affiliation, came much later, after Prohibition.) In New Orleans, his business associate might have sauntered up to the hotel bar and asked for the very same thing, made with either Kentucky bourbon or Pennsylvania rye. Cheers to the steamship.

*A quick geography refresher, if you (like us) enjoy that sort of thing: The Mississippi River begins at puny Lake Itasca in Minnesota. From there it flows south (and just a bit east), emptying into the Gulf of Mexico. Until the Louisiana Purchase, the Mississippi marked much of the western border of the United States. Over in Pittsburgh, the Monongahela and Allegheny Rivers flow together to form the Ohio River. The Ohio flows south and west, tumbling over the falls at Louisville (except that today it's not much of a falls, thanks to a man-made dam) and joining with the Mississippi at Cairo, Illinois (pronounced KAY-roe, if you were wondering, unlike the Egyptian capital) about 150 miles south of St. Louis. It's worth noting that the Mississippi River reaches its deepest point right by downtown New Orleans. Should you ever get a wild hair, after a night of cocktail "research" in the French Quarter, to hop in the river and swim over to Algiers Point—just don't.

Armagnac Sazerac

BEFORE THE SAZERAC was a rye cocktail, it was made with brandy. This drink balances the older French and newer American influences on the city of New Orleans and its cocktails. Armagnac, a kind of brandy, is native to the Gascony region of southwest France and usually has a lower price tag than its more famous cousin, cognac.

GARNISH:
Lemon peel

SERVICE ICE:
None

GLASS:
Coupe

YIELD: 1 (2½-ounce) cocktail

COCKTAIL:
⅛ ounce absinthe
1 ounce Armagnac
1 ounce bonded rye
⅛ ounce turbinado syrup, see recipe page 174 (simple syrup is an acceptable substitute)
4 dashes Peychaud's bitters
2 dashes barrel-aged bitters

Place crushed ice in a coupe, swirl to chill, and dump out. Replace the ice with the absinthe, swirl to coat the inside of the glass, and set aside. Combine the Armagnac, rye, turbinado syrup, and bitters in a mixing glass and stir. Strain into the prepared coupe, squeeze lemon peel over the surface of the drink, and place peel on the side of the glass.

Li'l Liza Jane

NAMED FOR THE New Orleans brass-band standard, this cocktail contains Crème Yvette, a liqueur made with berries and violet petals, resurrected in 2009 after being out of production for forty years. The slight purplish hue might remind you of the Mardi Gras color that represents justice. Cue up the Nina Simone recording of the song while you mix this drink, and sip slowly—it's more potent than it sounds.

GARNISH:
None

SERVICE ICE:
None

GLASS:
Coupe

YIELD: 1 (3¼-ounce) cocktail

COCKTAIL:
2 ounces bourbon, such as Eagle Rare
¾ ounce Crème Yvette
¼ ounce Herbsaint
3 dashes Peychaud's bitters

Place bourbon, Crème Yvette, Herbsaint, and bitters in a mixing glass, add ice, and stir. Strain into coupe.

The slight purplish hue might remind you of the Mardi Gras color that represents justice.

Rhythm and Soul

IF THE SOPHISTICATED RHYTHM of a well-stirred Manhattan was in a street fight
with the deep, heady soul of a Sazerac, we all know they'd make up later and fall in love.
This drink would be their love child, as imagined by its creator, Greg Best.

GARNISH:
Lemon peel

SERVICE ICE:
None

GLASS:
Rocks

YIELD: 1 (2¾-ounce) cocktail

COCKTAIL:
⅛ ounce absinthe

1½ ounces small-batch rye

½ ounce sweet vermouth, such as Cocchi di Torino

½ ounce amaro, such as Averna

4 dashes of Angostura bitters

Fill rocks glass with cracked ice, add absinthe, and set aside.
Combine rye, vermouth, amaro, and bitters in a mixing glass.
Add ice and gently stir until chilled. Roll the absinthe-and-ice
mixture around the inside of the rocks glass and pour out. Strain the
cocktail into the prepared glass and garnish with lemon peel.

Nite Tripper

CHRIS HANNAH, the bartender at Arnaud's French 75 bar in the French Quarter, used to walk around New Orleans with this smooth and boozy mix in his flask. When the legendary musician Mac Rebennack, a.k.a. Dr. John, a.k.a. the Night (or Nite) Tripper, tossed Hannah a Krewe du Vieux cup from a Mardi Gras parade float, he had a name for the drink. You could say he must have been in the right place at the right time.

Strega is an Italian aperitivo with sweet and savory notes. Look for the deep yellow color, which comes from saffron.

GARNISH:
Orange peel

SERVICE ICE:
None

GLASS:
Brandy snifter

YIELD: 1 (3-ounce) cocktail

COCKTAIL:
1¾ ounces bourbon
¾ ounce amaro, such as Averna
¼ ounce Strega
3 dashes Peychaud's bitters

Place bourbon, amaro, Strega, and bitters in a mixing glass. Add ice and stir. Strain into snifter, squeeze orange peel over drink, and place peel in snifter.

Martin Sawyer

WE HAVE NO BEEF with bright-eyed young bartenders. They're full of energy and eager to try new concoctions. The best ones can make a Tuesday night feel special, even if you just order a gin and tonic.

Here's a secret: The best bartenders retain those qualities no matter their age. Even if that age is north of eighty. Even if they've been behind the stick for six decades. Martin Sawyer was one of those bartenders. His life behind the bar offers us a telling story of the twentieth-century South.

Sawyer was born in New Orleans in 1921, the year Warren G. Harding was inaugurated twenty-ninth president of the United States. Prohibition was the law of the land. In the South, Jim Crow ruled the social order. At six, Sawyer saw the Mississippi River overrun the levees in the Great Flood of 1927. At fifteen, in the height of the Depression, he left school and began working as a grocery delivery boy, making a dollar a day.

During World War II, Sawyer found work at a New Orleans shipyard. A couple of years into the war, defense production slowed. Layoffs followed. A friend of Sawyer's worked at a French Quarter bar called the 500 Club. The only problem was, the friend couldn't read very well. Sawyer could. Did Sawyer want to come work with him as a barback—slicing fruit for garnishes, scooping ice, deciphering the orders from waitresses' notepads? Sawyer took the job.

He could read. And he had a keen eye and a sharp memory. Sawyer began learning the trade alongside his friend. Eventually he could make the all the drinks himself. Old-Fashioneds. Whiskey Sours. Tom Collinses. Pink Ladies and Grasshoppers. Sawyer was working at the 500 Club during Carnival in 1949, the year Louis Armstrong came home to ride in the parades as King of Zulu. Armstrong dropped in at the 500 Club and played a few numbers with the house band, the Basin Street Six. Sawyer had his picture made with Pops.

One night, Sawyer was called to define the color line. A group of would-be customers waited at the door. And there was a problem. They might be black. The manager couldn't tell for sure. So he found someone who would surely know. He sent Sawyer to the door. Sawyer looked at the group. They were definitely African American, same as him. He turned to the manager. "No, they're not black," he reported. The group was served, thanks to Sawyer's subversion.

From the 500 Club, Sawyer moved to the bar at the Casino Royal, a cabaret. From there he went to Brennan's. Then, as now, the white-tablecloth establishment drew hordes of tourists and locals alike for Sunday breakfast. Then, as now, cocktails flowed. Sawyer mixed Milk Punch and Bloody Marys in five-gallon batches to slake the thirst of 1,200 Sunday guests. For fifteen years he shook Gin Fizzes, too.

In 1971 Sawyer moved around the corner to the Rib Room at the Royal Orleans Hotel, where he would serve for the rest of his career. He could mix any drink a customer wanted, but he had a special way with Sazeracs and Mint Juleps. Somewhere along the line, Sawyer had learned that the original New Orleans Sazerac was made with brandy before rye took its place. So, with a nod to the old and the new, he made his Sazerac with brandy and rye.

He knew how to toss the glass with a flick of his wrist to distribute the anise-flavored liqueur in the glass. He expressed the lemon peel to make the surface of the drink "sparkle," as he put it, but he didn't rub the peel on the rim of the glass. If that hit of lemon oil is the first thing you taste, he explained, it diverts the palate.

Sawyer's Mint Julep was a thing of unconventional beauty. At the Rib Room he served it in a collins glass, perched on top of a cocktail napkin, cradled in a teacup saucer. When he wasn't in too much of a hurry, Sawyer often packed crushed ice *around* the glass while he was mixing the drink, so that the vessel got even colder. He muddled the mint and sugar, taking care not to muddle too hard, he said, because he didn't want you to catch flecks of mint in your straw. He mounded the ice and poured the bourbon, and finished the drink with a trifecta of garnishes: an orange slice, a maraschino cherry, and a sprig of fresh mint. The latter he frosted with a dusting of powdered sugar—an incongruous bit of snow in the subtropical Crescent City.

In 2005 Sawyer turned eighty-four years old. Thirty-four years into his tenure at the Rib Room, he was thinking about retirement. That August, Hurricane Katrina made the decision for him. Sawyer eventually returned to the city after the storm, but his bartending days were behind him. The Southern Foodways Alliance honored him with the 2005 Ruth Fertel Keeper of the Flame Award.

SCM

Pullman Porter

THIS IS A COMPLEX AND STRONG DRINK with both sweet and savory notes, named for the African American men who worked on railroad sleeping cars in the twentieth century. Though theirs were jobs defined by the contradictions of status and abuse, these men drove the rise of the black middle class and the advancement of the civil rights movement.

Suze is a low-proof French aperitif made with gentian root. While the recipe dates to the late nineteenth century, Suze has only recently been available in the United States.

GARNISH:
None

YIELD: 1 (3-ounce) cocktail

SERVICE ICE:
None

COCKTAIL:
1½ ounces 100-proof rye whiskey
¾ ounce Suze
¼ ounce simple syrup (see recipe page 174)

GLASS:
Rocks

⅛ ounce allspice liqueur, such as Pimento Dram

Place rye, Suze, simple syrup and allspice liqueur in a mixing glass. Add ice and stir. Strain into rocks glass.

Spaghetti Western

THE COMBINATION OF smoky mezcal, bitter Italian amaro, and sweet maraschino results in a balanced cocktail. But it's not for the faint of heart. Like an antihero in the Sergio Leone film *The Good, the Bad, and the Ugly*, this cocktail starts out rough. But if a stiff drink is what you need, it will save the day.

GARNISH:
None

SERVICE ICE:
None

GLASS:
Cocktail

YIELD: 1 (3½-ounce) cocktail

COCKTAIL:
1½ ounces mezcal, such as Del Maguey Vida
½ ounce 151-proof rum, such as Lemon Hart
½ ounce amaro, such as Nonino
¼ ounce Luxardo Maraschino
2 dashes Peychaud's bitters

Combine mezcal, rum, amaro, maraschino, and bitters in a mixing glass. Add ice and stir. Strain into cocktail glass.

The Spaghetti Western is not for the faint of heart.

9
Strong Finishes
Vieux Carré

Creolizing the Cocktail

The Vieux Carré is the most famous district of New Orleans. Within that precinct there is a place called the Hotel Monteleone. Within that grand hotel a bartender created what is, arguably, the most New Orleanian of New Orleans cocktails, the Vieux Carré.

You might wonder what would possess someone to introduce a new drink to the land of Sazeracs, Ramos Gin Fizzes, and French 75s. You might think, hey, I've barely heard of this Vieux Carré drink, what makes it so special?

Let's start with the history. The Monteleone Hotel, which opened in 1886, installed the rotating Carousel Bar and its twenty-five decorative stools in 1949. It makes a full rotation every fifteen minutes—just fast enough to make you wonder if the drinks are giving you the spins. Carousel seats fill up quickly with tourists and locals, but the view of Royal Street from a big leather chair by the window is just as charming. Late in the twentieth century, few patrons would have thought to order a Vieux Carré from either vantage point, but thanks the current cocktail renaissance, and the deft pours of bartender Marvin Allen, they are once again a menu staple. Mr. Allen says that his predecessor Walter Bergeron invented the drink in 1939.

The drink is equal portions of rye whiskey, cognac, and sweet vermouth, a small splash of the French herbal liqueur Bénédictine, highlighted by both Peychaud's and Angostura bitters. The formula shares some parallels with its ancestor the Sazerac. As with that drink, rye eventually replaced cognac when domestic liquors became more accessible than imported ones. Though the Louisiana legislature deemed the Sazerac New Orleans's official cocktail in 2008, doesn't the Vieux Carré's inclusive nature (including both rye and cognac, and both bitters), the creolization of cultures (French and American booze), and the flavorful touch of spice (French liqueur) sound a bit more like New Orleans?

Does being curiously representative of time and place make a drink better than its fellow New Orleanian classics? Of course not. But does it mean it should take—or, depending on your perspective, keep—its place in that cocktail pantheon? Absolutely.

JS

Vieux Carré

GARNISH:
Lemon peel

SERVICE ICE:
Cubed

GLASS:
Rocks

YIELD: 1 (3¼-ounce) cocktail

COCKTAIL:
1 ounce cognac
1 ounce rye whiskey
1 ounce sweet vermouth, such as Cocchi di Torino
¼ ounce Bénédictine
2 dashes Peychaud's bitters
2 dashes Angostura bitters

Place all ingredients in a mixing glass. Add ice and stir. Strain into ice-filled rocks glass. Squeeze lemon peel over drink and place peel in glass.

The Vieux Carré is the most New Orleanian of New Orleans cocktails.

The Old Square

"OLD SQUARE" is the literal English translation of Vieux Carré. This riff from Miles Macquarrie retains most of the standard Vieux Carré ingredients and proportions but subs Bonal Gentiane-Quina for the vermouth and calvados for the cognac. Bonal, a wine-based French aperitif, has less sweetness than vermouth and drinks like a light amaro. Calvados is a dry French apple brandy from Normandy. If you wanted to substitute a spirit from this side of the pond, you could use Laird's apple brandy (not applejack) from New Jersey.

GARNISH:
Lemon twist

SERVICE ICE:
Single large cube

GLASS:
Old-fashioned

YIELD: 1 (3-ounce) cocktail

COCKTAIL:
1 ounce rye whiskey
¾ ounce Bonal Gentiane-Quina
¾ ounce calvados
⅛ ounce Bénédictine
⅛ ounce Peychaud's bitters
4 dashes Angostura bitters

Place rye, Bonal, calvados, Bénédictine, and bitters in a mixing glass. Add some ice and stir. Strain into glass with large ice cube and garnish with lemon twist.

"Old Square" is the literal English translation of Vieux Carré.

Two-World Hero

THE MARQUIS DE LAFAYETTE was beloved for the roles he played in both the American and French Revolutions. In keeping with the eighteenth-century timeline, the black tea in this drink is a nod to the Boston Tea Party. Kellie Thorn of Empire State South in Atlanta created this drink prior to *Hamilton*-mania. As the song goes, "Everyone give it up for America's favorite fighting Frenchman!"

Note: Don't be scared off by the two subrecipes. Both are quick and easy to execute at home.

GARNISH:
Mint bouquet

SERVICE ICE:
Single large cube

GLASS:
Rocks

YIELD: 1 (2¾-ounce) cocktail

COCKTAIL:
1 ounce black-tea-infused cognac (see recipe below)
¾ ounce rye whiskey
¾ ounce sweet vermouth
¼ ounce red wine syrup (see recipe below)
1 dash Angostura bitters

Combine black-tea-infused cognac, whiskey, vermouth, red wine syrup, and bitters in a mixing glass. Add some ice and stir. Strain into chilled rocks glass with large ice cube and garnish with mint.

BLACK-TEA-INFUSED COGNAC
1 cup cognac
1 black tea bag

Combine cognac and tea bag in a glass, set aside for 10 minutes. Remove tea bag. Refrigerate cognac in an airtight container for up to 1 month.
Yield: 1 cup

RED WINE SYRUP
½ cup robust red wine, such as zinfandel
½ cup sugar

Combine wine and sugar in a bowl and stir until sugar dissolves. Refrigerate in an airtight container for up to 1 month.
Yield: Approximately ¾ cup

Cab Calloway

THIS BALANCED SHERRY-BASED SIPPER, from Tiffanie Barriere of Atlanta, is as smooth as the big band leader himself. Calloway grew up in western New York and Baltimore and attended law school in Chicago before becoming one of the most successful singers of his day. Between residences at Harlem's Cotton Club, he and his band toured the Jim Crow South on a charter train. Later Calloway played the supporting character Sportin' Life in a Broadway revival of *Porgy and Bess*, the George Gershwin opera set in Charleston. Be sure to keep this drink away from Minnie the Moocher.

GARNISH:
Lemon peel

SERVICE ICE:
Cubed

GLASS:
Rocks

YIELD: 1 (2½-ounce) cocktail

COCKTAIL:
1½ ounces dark sherry, such as oloroso
½ ounce rye whiskey
¼ ounce apricot liqueur
¼ ounce dry vermouth
2 dashes Angostura bitters
2 dashes orange bitters

Combine sherry, rye, apricot liqueur, vermouth, and bitters in a mixing glass. Add ice and stir. Strain into ice-filled rocks glass, squeeze lemon peel over the surface of the cocktail, and add peel to drink.

Negroni

THIS ITALIAN COCKTAIL has come to dominate the American cocktail imagination. We give you the original in order for you to be able to recognize its improvisations. The 1:1:1 ratio is easy to remember and has spawned dozens of spinoffs, some of which have become classics. Next time you're in Athens, Georgia, stop by Seabear Oyster Bar for a frozen Negroni slushy, which adds orange juice to the original. Thanks to the allure of the slush, Seabear claims the largest standing order for Campari in the state of Georgia.

GARNISH:
Orange peel

SERVICE ICE:
Cubed

GLASS:
Rocks

YIELD: 1 (3-ounce) cocktail

COCKTAIL:
1 ounce gin
1 ounce Campari
1 ounce sweet vermouth

Place gin, Campari, and sweet vermouth in a mixing glass. Add ice and stir. Strain into ice-filled glass, squeeze orange peel over drink, and place peel in glass.

An Endorsement for the Hotel Bar

CERTAIN HOTEL BARS have a character and a life all their own. They serve as havens and meeting spots for travelers and locals alike. Sociologist Ray Oldenburg coined the term "third place" to refer to vital public gathering places separate from home and work. Hotel bars can be just such spaces.

If we start in Louisville, in the upper reaches of the South, two examples spring to mind. The Lobby Bar at the Brown Hotel is a step back in time that is historically beautiful and unpretentiously welcoming. You can enjoy a drink in the opulent English Renaissance interior and not feel like an interloper. Order a bourbon or a Manhattan from the small oak-and-marble bar and settle into an overstuffed chair in the gilded two-story lobby. A certain thrill comes with drinking in such a storied space, one where local legends like Muhammad Ali and Hunter S. Thompson spent time.

At the opposite end of the spectrum is the Proof on Main bar at the 21c Museum Hotel. Ultramodern architecture, and a rotating collection of provocative modern art, is de rigueur for this growing hotel chain, which began in Louisville. This bar and restaurant was intended to stand on its own *and* be an amenity for the hotel. Visitors, residents, and the after-work crowd mingle in this highly visible corner bar.

Heading farther south, stops in two of Tennessee's grande dames, the Hermitage and the Peabody, give further credence to the hotel lobby bar as gathering spot for all. "Meet me at the Hermitage" was a phrase often spoken in twentieth-century Nashville. Today female bar patrons find an excuse to peek into the men's restroom for a glimpse of the green-and-black art deco décor. And the Peabody's Lobby Bar, with its evening parade of trained ducks making their way to the fountain, has been called "the living room of Memphis."

Farther down the Mississippi River from Memphis is New Orleans, where a myriad of hotel bars thrive in the town that essentially ignored Prohibition. Two, the Carousel Bar in the Hotel Monteleone and the Sazerac Bar at the Roosevelt, are where classic Southern cocktails were created or kept alive. A third, the Hot Tin Rooftop bar at the recently reopened Pontchartrain Hotel, nods to Tennessee Williams, who wrote *A Streetcar Named Desire* while living at the Pontchartrain.

We'll go so far as to declare that the hotel bar is experiencing a renaissance, and we suggest you take part in it. Visit a brand-new bar, or help breathe life into an old one. Try the roof of the Durham Hotel in Durham, North Carolina. Or The Living Room at the Dewberry in Charleston. Or Giardina's at the Alluvian in Greenwood, Mississippi. None of these hotel bars has the generic feel of a corporate hotel chain. They all share a sense of place, especially evocative of their city. For just the price of a cocktail, you get to participate in history, possibly art, and definitely community.

JS

Boulevardier

AN OBVIOUS COUSIN to the Negroni, this recipe appeared in Harry MacElhone's *Barflies and Cocktails* about ten years before the older Negroni was printed. MacElhone attributed this drink to his friend Erskine Gwynne. The American-in-Paris expat Gwynne was a nephew of Alfred Vanderbilt and ran a literary magazine called the *Boulevardier*.

GARNISH:
Orange peel

SERVICE ICE:
Cubed

GLASS:
Rocks

YIELD: 1 (3½-ounce) cocktail

COCKTAIL:
1½ ounces bourbon
1 ounce Campari
1 ounce sweet vermouth

Combine bourbon, Campari, and vermouth in a mixing glass. Add ice and stir. Strain into a rocks glass with ice. Squeeze orange peel over drink and place peel in glass.

The Boulevardier is an obvious cousin to the Negroni.

Savannah Rosa

NOT EVERYONE who walks into a bar is a craft cocktail expert. And that's fine with Matt McFerron at the Old Pal in Athens, Georgia. He enjoys introducing customers to new ingredients and cocktails by riffing on the classics. This recipe is a twist on the Boulevardier, but calls for Madeira in place of sweet vermouth and Aperol, an approachable alternative to Campari.

GARNISH:
Orange peel

SERVICE ICE:
None

GLASS:
Coupe

YIELD: 1 (3-ounce) cocktail

COCKTAIL:
1 ounce bourbon, such as Four Roses yellow label
1 ounce Madeira, such as Rare Wine Company's Savannah Verdelho
1 ounce Aperol
Rose water for misting

Stir bourbon, Madeira, and Aperol together with ice in a mixing glass. Strain into a coupe. Mist with rose water and garnish with an orange peel. (If you do not have a small spray bottle or atomizer to use as a mister, add 1 or 2 drops of rose water to the finished drink.)

Bitter Heart

THIS IS A BITTERSWEET Negroni variation that incorporates Cynar, an artichoke-based amaro, and amaretto, an almond-flavored liqueur. As Italian as the drink sounds, it is the brainchild of Atlanta-based bartender Navarro Carr. Enjoy one before you step out on the dance floor at the Sound Table, the bar-restaurant-DJ venue where Carr masterminds the cocktail offerings.

GARNISH:
Orange peel

SERVICE ICE:
Single large cube

GLASS:
Rocks

YIELD: 1 (3-ounce) cocktail

COCKTAIL:
1½ ounces Cynar
1 ounce gin
½ ounce amaretto

Place artichoke liqueur, amaretto, and gin in a mixing glass. Add some ice and stir. Strain into rocks glass with large ice cube and garnish with orange peel.

The Hardest Walk

BARTENDER AND EXPERIMENTAL MUSICIAN Turk Dietrich created this drink during his tenure at Cure in New Orleans. You'll recognize both the Manhattan and the Negroni in its bloodline, plus a nod to Louisiana's production of sugarcane. The drink takes its name from a song off the Jesus and Mary Chain's 1985 debut, *Psychocandy*. Cure proprietor Neal Bodenheimer calls it a "contemplative sipper," which is a sophisticated way of saying, "Drink slowly. This one packs a punch." If you're a Negroni fan, you're going to dig this one. Just enjoy responsibly, lest you find yourself doing the hardest walk—and feeling that distortion in your head.

GARNISH:
Orange peel

SERVICE ICE:
Cubed

GLASS:
Rocks

YIELD: 1 (3½-ounce) cocktail

COCKTAIL:
2 ounces vermouth, such as Punt e Mes
1 ounce aged overproof rum, such as Hamilton's
1/16 ounce Gran Classico
2 dashes orange bitters

Place vermouth, rum, Gran Classico, and bitters in glass.
Add ice and stir 30 revolutions. Squeeze orange peel over drink and place in glass.

The drink takes its name from a Jesus and Mary Chain song.

10

Enough to Go Around
Chatham Artillery Punch

Man Down

If the cocktail is the supreme American contribution to the drinking world, punch is Britain's gift. David Wondrich, who (literally) wrote the book on the subject, reckons that sailors cobbled the first punch together on voyages to and from the Indian subcontinent. Eventually the concoction found a home in English taverns. In the 1600s it crossed the pond to the Caribbean colonies as well as the North American mainland. Before long, punch became synonymous with Caribbean rum. That early rum was famously foul; watering it down and adding citrus, sugar, and spices helped to numb the burn.

Most drinkers agree that drinking is more fun with a crowd. Rotgut rum, even at room temperature, as it was served into the nineteenth century, isn't so bad when it becomes an excuse to get out of the house and pass a couple of hours in the company of friends. In the East Coast colonies, notes Wondrich, punch was an everyman drink, consumed by rags and riches types alike.

By the second half of the 1700s a greater variety of spirits gained popularity in England and the American colonies. During that time someone took punch a step further, mixing two or more liquors in a single bowl. Chatham Artillery Punch was born into this tradition. Created by a Savannah-based militia in the 1850s to toast another unit, the punch combines rum, brandy, and whiskey, with a generous pour of champagne. From the beginning it developed a reputation for being deceptively easy drinking, knocking even the hardiest soldiers on their rear ends.

Even as Chatham Artillery fired its first rounds, punch was already falling out of favor in the United States. "The down-the hatch, out-the-door-and-back-to-work" single-serving cocktail, as Wondrich puts it, gave the urban laborer just what he needed. Furthermore, substandard liquors became a thing of the past. Punch had once masked the bite of unaged rum. By the 1860s a properly mixed cocktail highlighted the virtues of domestic, aged bourbon or rye. Once an everyday, everyman drink, punch became a special-occasion treat.

Especially in the South, punch morphed from communal to clubby. There were (and still are) punches for Charleston debutante balls, punches for Richmond sporting clubs, punches for New Orleans carnival krewes. Polishing the bowl, unwrapping the glasses, muddling the lemon peels with sugar to release their oils: These became ritual aspects of private celebrations, often carried out by employees instead of celebrants.

Years ago the Southern Foodways Alliance revived the conviviality of the punch bowl, minus the exclusivity. We began with a scrubbed bathtub. Such a vessel is supremely democratic and capacious enough to serve a thirsty crowd of three hundred or so. At our annual symposium in Oxford, we often invite a guest bartender to fill the tub with a punch of his or her choice. Some have reclaimed archaic club concoctions for the assembled masses, while others have dreamed up their own concoctions. The tub, as much as its contents, unfailingly elicits smiles, conversations, and Instagrams. And, just as unfailingly, it causes more than a few of the attendees to turn up in sunglasses the next morning.

SCM

Chatham Artillery Punch

MANY VARIATIONS EXIST on Chatham Artillery Punch, all of them packing the wallop of multiple spirits, the tang of citrus, and the bubbles of sparkling wine. David Wondrich shares this version of the 1850s recipe in his book *Punch*. It's close to the original, but with ingredients you can easily find today. Don't be fooled by the versions on offer at tourist bars in Savannah; while intoxicating, they bear little resemblance to a true Chatham Artillery Punch.

GARNISH:
None

SERVICE ICE:
Crushed

GLASS:
Punch bowl and
punch cups

YIELD: 1¼ gallons

PUNCH:
1 recipe lemon oleo saccharum
1 pint freshly squeezed lemon juice
1 (750-milliliter) bottle VSOP cognac
1 (750-milliliter) bottle bourbon
1 (750-milliliter) bottle Jamaican-style rum
3 (750-milliliter) bottles chilled brut champagne

Mix oleo saccharum with lemon juice. Stir and strain into an empty 750-milliliter bottle. Add water to fill any remaining space in the bottle, seal, and refrigerate. At serving time, fill a two-and-a-half-gallon punch bowl with ice and pour in the bottled oleo saccharum. Add the bottles of cognac, bourbon, and rum. Top off with the 3 bottles of champagne. Stir before serving.

LEMON OLEO SACCHARUM
Peels of 12 lemons, with as little pith as possible
2 cups light raw sugar

Firmly muddle the peels in a sturdy bowl with the sugar. Cover and leave in a warm place for about 1 hour. Muddle again, and the mixture is ready to use.

Buford Highway Artillery Punch

THIS PUNCH takes Savannah's Chatham Artillery Punch as inspiration and gives it an Atlanta Global South twist in homage to suburban Atlanta's international corridor. Jerry Slater created it for the SFA's 2010 Buford Highway Field Trip. Tea was often an ingredient in early British and American punches; here the green tea is a nod to East Asia. The whiskey Slater chose for this recipe, High West Silver Oat, is an unaged white whiskey, but thanks to the oat, its bite is softer than a corn-based moonshine's. Shochu is a Japanese rice-based spirit, almost like a higher-proof sake. When Slater served the punch to SFA field trippers, he dressed the bowl with whole dragon fruits frozen in blocks of ice. You might want to do the same if you live near an Asian or international market that stocks dragon fruit. Lychees would work nicely, too.

GARNISH:
8 mint sprigs

SERVICE ICE:
Cubed ice from
punch bowl

GLASS:
Punch bowl and
punch cups

YIELD: ½ gallon, or 10 (3-ounce) servings, plus 2 quarts ice

PUNCH:
4 ounces unaged white whiskey, such as High West Silver Oat
4 ounces shochu, preferably rice based, such as Ginrei Shiro
6 ounces green tea, chilled
6 ounces lychee nectar or syrup from canned lychees
2 ounces ginger syrup (see recipe page 174)
4 dashes orange bitters
8 ounces sparkling wine

Place whiskey, sochu, green tea, lychee nectar, ginger syrup, bitters, and sparkling wine in a punch bowl. Add 2 quarts of ice and stir. Garnish with mint.

AWP 290 Punch

THIS WAS THE HOUSE PUNCH at H. Harper Station, Jerry and Krista Slater's bar and restaurant, housed in the former Atlanta–West Point train depot; 290 was the number of the train that hauled cotton from Atlanta to the textile mills in West Point, Georgia, near the Alabama border.

GARNISH:
5 mint sprigs

SERVICE ICE:
Ice ring or 1 quart large cubes

GLASS:
Punch bowl and punch cups

YIELD: 8 (3-ounce) servings

PUNCH:
5 ounces bourbon, such as Old Forester
3 ounces aged rum, such as Bacardi 8 Year
2 ounces peach nectar
2 ounces simple syrup (see recipe page 174)
2 ounces freshly squeezed lemon juice
4 ounces ginger beer
4 ounces soda water
9 mint sprigs, divided

Place bourbon, rum, peach nectar, simple syrup, lemon juice, and 4 mint sprigs in a shaker. Add ice and shake. Strain into a small punch bowl. Add ice ring or cubes. Add ginger beer and soda water, and garnish with remaining mint sprigs.

290 was the number of the train that hauled cotton from Atlanta to West Point, Georgia.

Watermelon Sangria

IN THE HEAT OF THE SUMMER, when watermelons are at their sweetest, this punch makes a party. The color is beautiful, and the sipping is easy. Just add friends.

GARNISH:
None

SERVICE ICE:
Ice ring and cubes

GLASS:
Punch bowl and
punch cups

YIELD: About 2 gallons

PUNCH:
1 whole medium-sized seedless watermelon, peeled and cubed
16 ounces dry London gin
8 ounces freshly squeezed lime juice
8 ounces agave syrup
1 handful fresh mint leaves
1 handful fresh thyme, large stems removed
4 bottles sparkling dry white wine, chilled

Place watermelon, gin, lime juice, agave syrup, mint leaves, and thyme in a 1-gallon container and set aside for at least 1 hour. When ready to serve, add chilled sparkling wine and ice ring. Serve over cubed ice.

Olde Thyme Punch

THIS IS A DELICIOUSLY BOOZY SIPPER, tropical and exotic. If you want to make one drink to impress the guests at your next party, this is it. Jayce McConnell named this punch for his friend Brandon Plyler, a beer nerd and spirits history buff everyone calls Old Time. It also pays homage to their home base of Charleston, where Madeira was once the wine of choice.

GARNISH:
Freshly grated nutmeg

SERVICE ICE:
Ice ring or cubed ice

GLASS:
Punch bowl and punch cups

YIELD: 1½ gallons

PUNCH:
1 recipe lemon, thyme, and nutmeg shrub (see recipe below)
1 (750-milliliter) bottle bourbon
1 (750-milliliter) bottle Madeira
½ bottle (375 milliliters) Jamaican rum, such as Smith & Cross
3 quarts water

Place shrub, bourbon, Madeira, rum, and water in a punch bowl. Add ice ring when ready to serve, or serve with ice in individual cups. Serve with additional freshly grated nutmeg.

LEMON, THYME, AND NUTMEG SHRUB
15 lemons
2 cups Demerara sugar
½ cup fresh thyme
2 whole grated nutmegs, about ¼ cup

Peel lemons, leaving behind as much pith as possible, and place peels in a nonreactive bowl. Add sugar, thyme, and nutmeg. Muddle mixture well, so that sugar coats the peels. Set aside to rest for 6 hours at room temperature or overnight in the refrigerator, stirring occasionally. Juice the leftover lemons and refrigerate juice. After the resting period, add lemon juice to peel mixture and stir until sugar is dissolved. Strain through a fine mesh strainer and refrigerate in an airtight container for up to 2 weeks.
Yield: Approximately 3 cups

Church Lady Punch

TEETOTALING IS A WAY OF LIFE for many Southerners. Since you are reading this book, chances are you're not one of them. But you probably know someone who is, for religious, health, or any number of other good reasons. And chances are, you've attended a party where you couldn't wait to get a drink in your hand—only to discover that alcohol wasn't being served. (Weddings, baby showers, and family reunions can be particularly challenging.) So when a stiff drink isn't an option, and the occasion calls for something more festive than iced tea, there's probably a punch bowl in sight. While we include only alcoholic recipes in this book, we would be remiss not to at least raise our glasses to the nonalcoholic punches that fill our region's community cookbooks.

In eighteenth-century England, and in colonial America, the drinkers gathered around the punch bowl would have been overwhelmingly male. By the mid-twentieth century, punch—especially the nonalcoholic kind—was a ladies' drink. Whereas rum punch was served in taverns, nonalcoholic punch was, and is, a drink for luncheons, showers, church socials, and funerals.

In the second half of the twentieth century, women's church groups and civic organizations published community cookbooks. These spiral-bound volumes showcased recipes for dishes from the everyday casserole to the holiday canapé, while raising money for charitable efforts. They were by no means exclusive to the South, but they were especially popular across the region. Typically divided into chapters by occasion, dish type, or base ingredient, many of these books devote at least a few pages to punch.

Church cookbooks tend to eschew alcohol entirely, while Junior League–sponsored volumes may include full-strength cocktails and punches. Attitudes toward alcohol also vary by geography and local culture; in *Charleston Receipts*, boozy punches and cocktails outnumber nonalcoholic ones five to one. In a cookbook from eastern Kentucky, on the other hand, you'd be hard pressed to find a punch recipe that calls for anything stronger than ginger ale.

In these Cold War–era concoctions, you can recognize the core components of rum punch from the pre-Revolutionary tavern. Citrus survives, often in the form of frozen orange juice, lemonade, or limeade concentrate. (More often than not, fresh fruits are spared in the making of these punches.) So does sugar—in unholy quantities. Spices and tea occasionally appear in ingredient lists, but most of these recipes forgo complexity for simple, fruity sweetness. In blessed contrast to the tavern punches of the colonial era, these punches are iced—often creatively. One 1970s recipe called for a frozen ring mold of carbonated Tom Collins mixer. (This product seems to have disappeared from the market years ago, but its memory lives on among its dedicated fans, who commiserate and discuss acceptable substitutes on Internet message boards.)

Juices, too, could be frozen into punch ice. Some recipes call for freezing the entire mixture, then thawing it to a slushy consistency before serving. In such cases, carbonated ingredients are added at party time. Sherbet is a near constant. It might be a twentieth-century addition to the punch bowl. But there's a more intriguing possibility. Historically, explains David Wondrich, the citrus-sugar amalgam at the base of almost all punches was called "shrub" or "sherbet." Could it be that a midcentury hostess got hold of an archival punch recipe and interpreted "sherbet" as the fruity frozen dessert? We kind of hope so.

A number of social and culinary factors likely paved the way for the garish punches of the mid-twentieth century. In cities and suburbs, middle-class women had leisure time on their hands. Especially if they didn't work full time, they were likely to make civic engagements into social gatherings. Punch fueled these female spaces. At a Junior League luncheon or a garden club meeting, nonalcoholic punch tasted just right: festive without being scandalous. It didn't hurt that it was a pretty color, made with commercial ingredients like powdered Jell-O or concentrated limeade that telegraphed middle-class status. A hostess in 1965 would fill her heirloom crystal or silver punch bowl with ingredients that didn't exist in her grandmother's time.

Is there a place for nonalcoholic punch in the twenty-first century, the era of the female CEO and the boozy girls' night out? Search "punch" or "party punch" on Pinterest, and you find dozens of recipes. The one that calls for gummy worms encased in frozen cubes of Hawaiian Punch is presumably intended for a children's party, not a ladies' luncheon. But in certain settings, the classics hang on. After a 2015 funeral in Sanford, North Carolina, the women of the First Presbyterian Church laid out a light spread for the congregation. There were cookies and sandwiches, a hodgepodge of store-bought and homemade. The fried chicken and ham biscuits would come out later, at the home of the deceased. So would the Mimosas and the Bloody Marys. Here, in the annex between the sanctuary and the recreation hall, punch held court.

It was straight out of a ladies' auxiliary cookbook: Nearly fluorescent green, the surface foam a tip-off that lime sherbet was the coloring agent. And it was tooth-achingly sweet. The deceased had preferred scotch. Born in 1922, she had earned a master's degree, taught music, raised three sons, and outlived three husbands. She would have smiled in recognition at that first sip of punch.

SCM

Twelfth Night Punch

EPIPHANY, the twelfth night of Christmas, is the start of Carnival season in New Orleans. On January 6, when the weather is cool and memories of the holiday season still linger, this spiced bourbon-and-port punch is great way to launch the next season. The color, a ruby-esque red-pink, is gorgeous, and the flavor is like that of mulled wine, but spicier and more complex. Happy holidays.

GARNISH:
Freshly grated
nutmeg

SERVICE ICE:
Ring or cubes

GLASS:
Punch bowl and
punch cups

YIELD: 6 to 8 servings

PUNCH:
14 ounces bourbon
8 ounces freshly squeezed lemon juice
8 ounces ruby port
3 ounces allspice liqueur, such as Pimento Dram
4 ounces orgeat
4 ounces black tea
Peel of 1 lemon
Peel of 1 orange
12 cloves

Combine first six ingredients in a pitcher and chill. Stud the lemon and orange peels with the cloves and set aside. When guests arrive, pour the contents of the pitcher into a punch bowl, add ice, add the studded lemon and orange peels, and stir. Generously grate nutmeg over the punch bowl and again over each cup when serving.

Chinese Grocery Five-Treasures Punch

DAVID WONDRICH created this punch as a variation on the nineteenth-century Mississippi Punch, renaming it with a nod to the Chinese immigrants who owned and operated grocery stores in twentieth-century Delta towns. Wondrich hopes that Southern distillers will experiment in the future with sorghum. At present the only country that goes deep into beverage sorghum is China, where the resulting spirit is *baijiu*, or "white wine." This bears approximately the same relation to sauvignon blanc that a saber-toothed tiger does to an elderly, declawed lap kitty. Funky (an understatement), fruity, dry, and very strong, baijiu is what Wondrich calls the blue cheese of the spirits world.

GARNISH:
None

SERVICE ICE:
Ring

GLASS:
Punch bowl and
punch cups

YIELD: 10 small servings

PUNCH:
6 ounces Kinmen Kaoliang 58 percent baijiu*

6 ounces Jamaican rum, such as Smith & Cross

6 ounces high-proof bourbon

6 ounces sorghum simple syrup (made by mixing equal parts thick
    sorghum syrup or sorghum molasses, such as Muddy Pond,
    and water)

6 ounces freshly squeezed lime juice

Combine all ingredients, shake over ice—in batches if you do not have a large enough shaker—and strain into ice-filled punch bowl.

*A note on using baijiu: For this, you don't want baijiu at its funkiest. Kweichow Moutai, the flagship brand, is that, and wonderful in its way, but it would move into this drink, take over, and kick every other ingredient out on the street. Kaoliang, from Taiwan, still has the funk, and plenty of it, but it can play with others.

Vishwesh Bhatt's Cocktail Bites

(Or, Never Drink on an Empty Stomach)

Snackbar in Oxford, Mississippi, is one of the SFA's de facto staff bars. Its cocktail program can go toe to toe with the top dogs in the region, and it's hands down the best food and drink you'll enjoy in a small-town strip mall anchored by a Cold War–era Sears. Proprietor John Currence and chef Vishwesh Bhatt conceived Snackbar as a Southern brasserie: upscale bar food with a French accent, a raw bar, and great cocktails, wine, and beer. It's all of those things. Over the years, Bhatt, who grew up in the Indian state of Gujarat, has brought more of his own tastes to his adopted Mississippi home. Think catfish tikka masala. Ginger-and-turmeric-spiced boiled peanut slaw. Gulf shrimp in a chili-lime-coconut broth.

Because Snackbar is inseparable from its drink list, Bhatt knows cocktail munchies. So we asked him to share some of his favorites with us—dips, bites, and finger foods that you can make at home, with ingredients that aren't impossible to find. These recipes are batched to serve a cocktail party of about eight to twelve adults who have dinner plans afterwards. All of them show a little saltiness, the better to go with alcohol of any sort. Most can and should be made ahead, Bhatt says, so that you can join the party rather than worrying about the food.

Benedictine Spread

THIS IS A SLIGHTLY UNORTHODOX take on a Kentucky classic, a fresher and more natural (note the absence of green food coloring) version of the original. Even though Bhatt graduated from the University of Kentucky, he doesn't remember coming across this recipe until he saw the Kentucky chef Ouita Michel serve it at a festival. It reminded him of the tea sandwiches of cucumber and cream cheese that his mother used to serve to guests in India, a custom borrowed from the British.

YIELD: 3½ cups

2 medium cucumbers, peeled, seeded, and minced
½ cup minced red onion
1 teaspoon salt, plus more if desired
8 ounces cream cheese, at room temperature
8 ounces mascarpone cheese, at room temperature
2 teaspoons chopped fresh dill
2 teaspoons chopped fresh parsley
1 jalapeño, seeded and minced
½ teaspoon freshly ground black pepper

Place the cucumbers and onions in a mixing bowl lined with cheesecloth or a tea towel, sprinkle with the salt, and gently toss. Set aside for 30 minutes, then gather the edges of the cheesecloth and squeeze out as much liquid as possible. Discard the liquid and return the cucumber mixture to the mixing bowl. Add the cheeses, dill, parsley, jalapeño, and black pepper and gently stir to combine. Refrigerate in an airtight container for no more than 2 days. Serve as a sandwich spread or dip.

Catfish Rillettes

Like many dishes at Snackbar, this recipe shows dual influences. You can look at it as a gussied-up version of the smoked fish dips of the Gulf Coast (catfish or mullet is often the fish of choice), or as a spread that walked off the charcuterie board at a French brasserie and took a trip through the Mississippi Delta. Catfish is much leaner than the pork or salmon with which rillettes are usually made. Cream cheese, bacon fat, and butter hold this recipe together, making it rich and spreadable. Serve it with crackers or crusty bread.

YIELD: 4 cups

1½ pounds catfish filets, cleaned and patted dry (Snackbar uses Simmons
    Farm Raised Catfish)
1 tablespoon Creole seasoning
2 teaspoons kosher salt, divided, plus more if desired
½ cup bacon grease
¼ cup unsalted butter
1 tablespoon minced garlic
½ cup white wine
2 tablespoons freshly squeezed lemon juice
½ tablespoon Worcestershire sauce
1½ teaspoons dried thyme
¼ teaspoon cayenne pepper
8 ounces cream cheese, at room temperature

Preheat the oven to 375°F.

Place the catfish on a parchment-lined sheet pan and sprinkle with Creole seasoning and 1 teaspoon of the salt. Bake for 6 to 7 minutes or until opaque and just cooked through. Set aside to cool slightly.

Place the bacon grease, butter, and garlic in a large sauté pan and set over medium heat. Cook 3 to 4 minutes until the fat has melted and the garlic has softened and is becoming lightly golden. Add the catfish, the remaining teaspoon of salt, wine, lemon juice, Worcestershire, thyme, and cayenne pepper and simmer, stirring occasionally, until the catfish is falling apart and much of the liquid has evaporated, 25 to 30 minutes.

Remove from the heat and cool to room temperature, then stir in the cream cheese until the mixture is well blended and has a spreadable consistency. Taste and adjust the seasoning. Transfer to a glass jar with a lid and store in the refrigerator for up to 2 weeks.

Deviled Pickled Eggs

Credit for this recipe goes to John Currence. Currence was probably inspired by the gallon jars of pickled eggs that are counter fixtures at country gas stations in Mississippi. Pickling the eggs gives you a more flavorful deviled egg. But Snackbar didn't stop there. "Putting a deviled egg on the menu was sort of cheating," admits Bhatt. "We wanted to elevate it a little bit." Lump crab did the trick. "We always have crabmeat in-house for the seafood platter, so we decided to add it to the deviled eggs." The sour cream–mayonnaise–cream cheese combo is a little more fussy than the standard deviled egg filling, but it cuts the graininess of the yolk, providing a smoother texture and a nicer mouthfeel. If you don't have two days to let the eggs sit in the pickling brine, you can use regular boiled eggs.

YIELD: 24 egg halves

12 pickled eggs (see recipe below)
8 ounces lump crabmeat, picked
⅓ cup minced chives
¼ cup minced celery
¼ cup sour cream
2 tablespoons cream cheese, at room temperature
2 tablespoons mayonnaise, at room temperature
2 tablespoons Creole mustard
2 tablespoons freshly squeezed lemon juice
1 tablespoon Tabasco
1 teaspoon cayenne pepper
¾ teaspoon kosher salt

Slice the pickled eggs in half lengthwise. Gently remove the yolks and transfer them to a large mixing bowl. Set the whites aside. Mash the yolks with a fork until smooth, add the remaining ingredients, and gently stir to combine. Fill the egg white halves with the mixture. Serve immediately.

PICKLED EGGS

12 eggs

2½ cups red wine vinegar

½ cup dry white wine

1 small red onion, sliced

1 teaspoon kosher salt

4 cloves garlic, sliced

2 teaspoons red pepper flakes

3 whole cloves

3 bay leaves

½ tablespoon paprika

¼ cup chopped fresh parsley

¼ cup sliced green onion tops

Place the eggs in a medium saucepan and cover with water by 1 inch. Bring to a boil over high heat. As soon as the water boils, remove from the heat, cover, and set aside for 12 minutes. Drain and rinse under cold water until cool enough to handle. Peel the eggs, transfer them to a large nonreactive container, and set aside to cool.

Combine the vinegar, white wine, red onion, salt, garlic, red pepper, cloves, bay leaves, and paprika in a small saucepan. Place over high heat and bring to a boil. Pour the hot liquid over the eggs. Add the parsley and the green onions. Cover and refrigerate for at least 2 days before using.

Deviled Ham

DON'T CONFUSE THIS with the tinned stuff on the convenience-store shelf. Snackbar uses Benton's ham from Madisonville, Tennessee. If you've ever had Benton's, you know it would be sacrilege to let it go to waste. So after slicing the ham for Monte Cristo sandwiches, Bhatt gives the end pieces new life as a dip. He likes to taste-test it on white bread; saltines are an appropriate pairing, too.

YIELD: Approximately 3½ cups

1 pound good-quality country ham, coarsely chopped
4 ounces cream cheese, at room temperature
4 ounces fresh goat cheese, at room temperature
½ cup mayonnaise
1 tablespoon Creole mustard
1 teaspoon dry mustard
½ teaspoon cayenne pepper
2 green onions, coarsely chopped
¼ cup fresh parsley leaves, slightly packed
1 tablespoon Tabasco
½ teaspoon freshly ground black pepper
Pinch of kosher salt, plus more if desired

Place all ingredients in the bowl of a food processor and pulse until finely chopped, stopping to scrape down the sides of the bowl as needed. Taste and adjust seasoning. Refrigerate in an airtight container for up to 1 week.

Okra Chaat

OKRA IS AS BELOVED on the Indian subcontinent as it is in the American South. This is an Indian-street-food-inspired twist on fried okra—many Southerners' favorite way to eat the stuff. Whereas meat-and-three fried okra is often enveloped in a thick batter, this version uses no batter at all, letting the okra shine. It borrows from a North Indian dish called subir saran. Serve as a finger food or on a small plate.

YIELD: 8 to 10 appetizer servings

¼ cup freshly squeezed lime juice
1 teaspoon sugar
3 Roma tomatoes, diced
3 medium shallots, peeled and thinly sliced
2 serrano peppers, thinly sliced, seeds removed if desired
½ cup chopped cilantro
1 tablespoon chaat masala, divided
½ teaspoon cayenne pepper
3 pounds okra, thinly sliced lengthwise
Salt
1 cup roasted peanuts, coarsely chopped
Peanut oil for frying

Combine the lime juice and sugar in a large mixing bowl and stir until sugar dissolves. Add the tomatoes, shallots, serrano peppers, cilantro, ½ tablespoon of the chaat masala, and cayenne pepper and stir to combine. Set aside.

Heat 1 inch of peanut oil in a large Dutch oven or heavy pot, to 375°F. Carefully add the okra in small batches and fry until light golden brown and crispy, 2 to 3 minutes. Transfer to a sheet pan lined with paper towels, season with salt, and cool. Repeat until all of the okra has been fried.

To serve, add the okra and peanuts to the tomato mixture and gently toss to combine. Divide the mixture into serving portions and sprinkle with the remaining chaat masala.

Eugene Walter

A GOOD DRINK TASTES BEST when served by a talented host. Eugene Walter, a native of Mobile, Alabama, who distinguished himself during the mid-twentieth century as a writer and lyricist and provocateur, may have been the best host to ever set a Southern table or lean against a sub-Mason-Dixon bar.

His voice was thick with honey and mud, a brogue born of the land where he was reared. In his youth, Eugene Walter's blue eyes flashed with a perverse glee. In later years, a shock of white hair framed his wide face. Though he loved his native region, he banned to a lower circle of hell the "so-called moral majority," which he declared to be "neither moral nor majority."

Walter regarded Mobile as a place out of time, where he witnessed "the end of the 18th Century and the beginning of the 22nd." In his writings, the city was a character, a palpable and constant presence. "Down in Mobile they're all crazy," he wrote in his novel *An Untidy Pilgrim*, "because the Gulf Coast is the kingdom of monkeys, the land of clowns, ghosts and musicians, and Mobile is sweet lunacy's county seat."

Walter moved to Europe after World War II. But he didn't leave Mobile behind. Under his bed he stashed a good-luck shoebox of red clay dug from a gully near his birthplace. On his terrace he tended a patch of okra. On a plot of land near the Coliseum, he planted collards.

A man of letters, Walter contributed an essay to the first issue of the *Paris Review* and served as an advisory editor for nearly ten years. In Rome in the 1960s and 1970s, he worked as a translator for Federico Fellini and acted in his films, including *8½* and *Juliet of the Spirits*.

Visitors to Rome sought two audiences then: the pope and Eugene Walter. An inventive cook and a celebrated storyteller with a reputation for rococo embroidery, his watchword as a host was "The dinner table is the sunburst from which ideas go orbiting." During a party at his apartment on the Corso Vittorio Emanuele, he once crafted a stained-glass window out of gumdrops for Fellini. At another gathering, he dished a platter of black-eyed peas and ham hocks for two princesses as a parade of cats sashayed along a table runner set with Silly Putty centerpieces.

When Walter returned to Mobile to roost in January of 1979, his social patterns changed. "I stay close to home most of the time," he told Denise Gee, "unless, of course, someone's buying dinner, and then I'm a boy with bells on. Otherwise I simply rise and do a bit of sonnet writing, then take a nap, then eat a little, read a little, and then, when there's an emergency—and there most always is—I fill my bathtub up with Jim Beam and swim my way to safety."

Later in his life, Walter turned his literary attentions to food and drink, a topic he had written about only occasionally during his years abroad. In 1984 he published *Delectable Dishes from Termite Hall: Rare and Unusual Recipes*, a treasure trove of arcana like Patent Leather Pie (a tuna casserole topped with baked-black eggplant slices) and mace-spiked black-eyed pea patties. Next came *Hints and Pinches: A Concise Compendium of Herbs, Spices, and Aromatics with Illustrative Recipes and Asides on Relishes, Chutneys, and Other Such Concerns*, brightened with Walter's drawings of mango-eating monkeys, dancing cats, and anthropomorphic garlic bulbs.

As the years rolled on, he planned more food and drink books, including *Dixie Sips and Dixie Sups and Sometimes We're Quite Reasonable*. Supplemented by a few previously published recipes and texts, the manuscript for that book became *The Happy Table of Eugene Walter*. Published posthumously in 2011, it's a roster of dishes made with spirituous liquors. It's also a showcase of an ever spirituous Eugene Walter, who, in often baroque and always entertaining prose, paid homage to the possibilities of strong drink, writing, "If I were really wealthy, I'd create a bar with a bartender named Misty and a bar list with 200 versions, at the least, of the julep."

JTE

Pickled Shrimp

THE BETTER THE SHRIMP, the better this recipe will be. If you live near a coast, choose the shrimp that made the shortest trip from the water to your local market. In Mississippi, that means Gulf shrimp. Snackbar gets theirs from Gollott's, a fourth-generation seafood business out of D'Iberville, Mississippi. Depending on the formality of your gathering, serve these with forks, with toothpicks, or as a finger food.

YIELD: 2 quarts

2 pounds large (21/25 count) headless, peeled shrimp

2 quarts plus ¾ cup water

¼ cup white wine

1 tablespoon kosher salt

3 bay leaves, divided

1 lemon, thinly sliced

1 small red onion, thinly sliced

2 teaspoons whole black peppercorns

1 teaspoon red pepper flakes

10 cloves garlic, sliced

2½ cups apple cider vinegar

1 tablespoon mustard seeds, crushed

2 tablespoons sugar

2 tablespoons minced ginger

1½ teaspoons Tabasco

Rinse the shrimp and set aside. Prepare an ice bath. Place 2 quarts water, wine, salt, 1 bay leaf, and 2 lemon slices in a large pot. Bring to a boil, add the shrimp, and cook 30 to 40 seconds. Remove shrimp, strain, and shock in the ice bath to stop the cooking. Transfer the shrimp to a large glass mixing bowl and set aside.

Place the remaining bay leaves, remaining lemon slices, onion, peppercorns, pepper flakes, garlic, vinegar, mustard seed, sugar, ginger, and Tabasco in a small saucepan with ¾ cup water. Place over medium-high heat and bring to a simmer. Remove from the heat and cool for 5 minutes. Pour the mixture over the shrimp and stir to combine. Cover and refrigerate for at least 4 hours and up to overnight before serving. Store in refrigerator for up to 1 week.

Shrimp Toast

BHATT LOVES SHRIMP TOAST, a dish that's popular in parts of Vietnam and China. To serve that toast made with Gulf shrimp at a Mississippi restaurant is to embrace the twenty-first-century South, in which new immigrants apply skills and foodways to their adopted homes. Many of the shrimpers and seafood packers working on the Gulf Coast today are first- or second-generation Vietnamese Americans.

YIELD: 8 to 10 servings

1 pound large (25/30 count) headless, peeled shrimp, rinsed and coarsely chopped
½ teaspoon kosher salt
½ teaspoon freshly ground black pepper
1 whole egg
2 green onions, coarsely chopped
2 cloves garlic, peeled and coarsely chopped
1 tablespoon chopped fresh ginger
1 teaspoon sesame oil
Zest of 1 lime
1 teaspoon chopped fresh mint, plus extra for garnish
½ tablespoon soy sauce
½ tablespoon fish sauce
1 teaspoon cornstarch
1 loaf French bread, cut into ½-inch-thick slices
1 to 2 teaspoons olive oil
Fresh chopped basil, for garnish
Toasted sesame seeds, for garnish

Place the shrimp, salt, pepper, egg, onions, garlic, ginger, sesame oil, zest, mint, soy sauce, and fish sauce in the bowl of a food processor. Pulse until chopped fine and well combined. Transfer to a mixing bowl and stir in the cornstarch.

Spread a generous amount of the shrimp paste on each slice of bread. Heat a small amount of oil in a sauté pan until shimmering. Add 3 to 4 slices of bread, shrimp side down, to the pan and cook until golden brown, 2 to 3 minutes. (The protein in the shrimp creates a sticky paste, so it really adheres to the bread. You don't have to worry that it will fall off in the pan.) Flip and cook until bread is golden brown and crispy, 1 to 2 minutes. Repeat with remaining pieces. Garnish with mint, basil, and sesame seeds and serve immediately.

Snackbar Pimento Cheese

THE SFA ONCE MADE thirteen and a half gallons of pimento cheese for a symposium and published a companion cookbook with more than 175 PC recipes. So yeah, when we serve cocktails, you can bet we're serving pimento cheese. Snackbar shares our values. Their version is a slightly elevated take on the original. The caraway reminds Bhatt of a tinned cheese flavored with cumin and caraway that he ate as a child.

YIELD: 5 cups

1 large red bell pepper
¼ cup pimientos, drained
4 ounces cream cheese, at room temperature
1 pound sharp white cheddar, shredded
1 cup mayonnaise
1 teaspoon Tabasco
½ teaspoon sugar
¼ teaspoon cayenne pepper
¼ teaspoon ground white pepper
¼ teaspoon smoked paprika
¼ cup finely chopped pickled red onions
¼ cup finely chopped bread-and-butter pickles
¾ teaspoon toasted caraway seeds

Heat oven to 450°F.

Place the bell pepper in an aluminum-foil-lined pan and roast 40 to 50 minutes or until wrinkled and charred, turning once or twice. Remove from the oven, enclose completely in foil, and set aside to cool. Once cool enough to handle, remove the skin, stem, and seeds and finely chop. Place the chopped pepper in a large mixing bowl, add the remaining ingredients, and stir to combine. Refrigerate in an airtight container for up to 1 week.

Spicy Crunchy Black-Eyed Peas

THIS IS A RIFF ON one of Bhatt's favorite Indian street snacks, chana jor garam, made with flattened fried chickpeas. After a recent trip to India, Bhatt came home and tinkered with the formula. He discovered that frying black-eyed peas adds an awesome texture and flavor. For a cocktail party, serve individual portions in paper cones. That's how street vendors sell chana jor garam in Bhatt's home city of Ahmedabad.

YIELD: 8 to 10 appetizer servings

2 cups dried black-eyed peas
1 tablespoon kosher salt, plus more as desired
Pinch of turmeric, optional
½ cup minced red onion
2 Roma tomatoes, seeded and diced small
½ cup small-diced cucumber
1 serrano pepper, seeded and minced
⅓ cup lightly packed chopped fresh cilantro
¼ cup lightly packed chopped mint
Juice of 2 limes
2 teaspoons chaat masala
½ teaspoon sugar
½ teaspoon cayenne pepper
Peanut oil for frying

Place the peas, salt, and turmeric, if using, in a 4-quart saucepan. Add enough water to cover the peas by 1 inch, place over high heat, and bring to a boil. Decrease the heat to maintain a simmer and cook until the peas are just tender, about 40 minutes. Drain well and set aside to cool.

Combine the onion, tomatoes, cucumber, serrano pepper, cilantro, mint, lime juice, chaat masala, sugar, and cayenne in a large mixing bowl and set aside.

Heat 1 inch of peanut oil in a large Dutch oven or heavy pot, to 360°F. Carefully add the peas in small batches and fry until light golden brown and crispy, 3 to 4 minutes. Transfer to a sheet pan lined with paper towels and season with salt. Repeat until all of the peas have been fried. Set aside to cool to room temperature.

Once cool, add the fried peas to the onion-tomato mixture, toss to combine, and serve immediately.

Note: This recipe also works well if you substitute roasted, unsalted peanuts for the black-eyed peas.

Sweet Potato, Ham, and Cheese Biscuits

BHATT AND HIS MISSISSIPPI IN-LAWS share a love of sweet-salty flavor combinations. Every year at Thanksgiving, his father-in-law makes a casserole of baked sweet potatoes with cinnamon, brown sugar, and chopped bacon. That dish inspired these biscuits. So did the high-holy appetizer of the Southern hostess: biscuits with country ham. For this recipe, Bhatt put the ham *in* the biscuit dough. You can thank him next time you see him.

You don't have to make the pear jam to serve with these biscuits, but you should. It's inspired by murrabbo, a classic Indian green mango preserve. Between the ham-studded biscuits and the fruit jam, Bhatt says, you've almost got a Southern riff on a Monte Cristo.

YIELD: Approximately 28 biscuits

1¾ cups all-purpose flour, plus extra for rolling dough

1 tablespoon brown sugar

1 tablespoon baking powder

½ teaspoon baking soda

1 teaspoon kosher salt

6 tablespoons unsalted butter, chilled and cubed

½ cup finely diced country ham

1 jalapeño, seeded if desired, minced

1 tablespoon orange zest

¾ cup mashed sweet potato, chilled

½ cup sharp cheddar, shredded

1 whole egg

⅓ cup buttermilk

Heat oven to 400°F.

Whisk together the flour, brown sugar, baking powder, baking soda, and salt in a large bowl. Using your fingertips, rub the butter into the flour mixture until crumbly. Stir in the ham, jalapeño, and orange zest. In a separate bowl, whisk together the sweet potato, cheese, egg, and buttermilk. Fold into the flour mixture to form a soft dough.

Turn the dough out onto a floured work surface and fold it over on itself 6 to 8 times. Roll dough to ½-inch thickness and cut out 2½-inch rounds. Reroll and cut until all dough is used. Place biscuits on a sheet pan just touching each other. Bake for 10 to 12 minutes or until light golden. Remove to a rack to cool. Serve with pear jam (recipe follows).

Pear Jam with Saffron and Cardamom (Murrabbo)

THIS JAM would also be good with cheese straws, over goat cheese on a cracker, or by itself on toast. All that, and you don't even have to sterilize a Ball jar.

YIELD: 1 quart

3 pounds (about 6 or 7) Bartlett pears, peeled, cored, and diced
2 cups sugar
¾ cup honey
1 cinnamon stick
5 whole cloves
2 cardamom pods
2 healthy pinches saffron
1 teaspoon kosher salt

Combine all the ingredients in a large, heavy pot. Place over medium-low heat and cook, stirring frequently, for 1½ to 2 hours, until thick and deep golden in color. Remove from heat, skim off the foam, and set the pot in an ice bath to chill. Remove the cinnamon, cloves, and cardamom. Transfer the jam to a glass jar and store in the refrigerator for up to 1 month.

Tools

You don't have to have every one of these tools of the trade in your home bar arsenal, but they certainly help. Start with the gadgets that elevate your favorite drink, and build from there.

Atomizer for spritzing a fragrant spirit, such as absinthe, mezcal, or Islay scotch, into the glass before or after a cocktail is poured.

Bar Spoon for stirring cocktails. Various sizes and materials are available. Make sure the one you choose has a tightly spiraled handle. Avoid any with red plastic tips that mask a rough finish at the end of the handle.

Boston Shaker, a two-piece metal or metal-and-glass shaker that fits together to form a seal

Channel Knife for making long, thin citrus garnishes

Citrus Squeezer (Juicer) for small amounts. For larger batches, consider a manual or electric citrus press.

Cobbler Shaker, a three-piece shaker with a built-in strainer

Conical or Fine Mesh Strainer for use in tandem with the Hawthorne strainer to "double-strain" or "fine-strain," insuring no ice chips or other matter make it into the cocktail.

Grater such as the Microplane brand. In addition to nutmeg, one with fine holes can tackle cinnamon, citrus zest, etc.

Hawthorne Strainer with spring for trapping ice, fruit, or other additives. Used with Boston shaker to strain shaken drinks.

Jiggers to measure ingredients. Most standard jiggers are dual purpose, measuring 1 ounce on one side and 2 ounces on the other. There should be rings on the inside of the jigger to measure smaller amounts.

Julep Strainer for use with a mixing glass to strain stirred cocktails

Lewis Bag to make crushed ice. This canvas bag, used in conjunction with a wooden mallet, keeps ice dry.

Mixing Glass for stirred drinks. The better versions are designed with a convex bottom so that a spoon glides around when stirring.

Muddler for pressing or grinding (muddling) herbs, citrus, sugars, etc. A wooden muddler of substantial size will get the job done efficiently.

Nutmeg Grater for grating nutmeg onto cocktails. Buy one in which you can conveniently store a whole nutmeg in the top.

Paring Knife for cutting citrus and the like. Keep it sharp.

Silicone Ice Molds in various sizes for making uniform cubes. Ice slips out of these molds more easily than plastic trays.

Tap-Icer, a tool created by Frank Earnest in the 1940s to crack large ice cubes into small pieces

Wine Key, not a cocktail tool per se, but always good to have around

Y-Peeler for making citrus peel garnishes

Techniques

Building Whether making a stirred or a shaken drink, add your ingredients to the vessel before adding the ice. This way, no ingredient becomes too diluted.

Citrus Peel Garnish, or "Express Yourself" This is the most commonly used garnish technique in classic and neoclassic cocktails. Using a Y-shaped vegetable peeler, shave a wide swath of peel, about 1 by 3 inches. Using both hands, grab the peel with your thumb and first two fingers. Point the peel, skin side out, at the glass, and squeeze. This should spray a fine mist of citrus oil over the cocktail. Discard the peel at this point or, to intensify the flavor, rub the edge of the glass with the peel and drop it into the cocktail.

Citrus Spiral This long, thin citrus garnish looks great cascading down a champagne glass or tied in a knot and hanging languidly off a cocktail glass. Using a channel knife, make a spiraling cut in the fruit. Start at one end of your citrus and rotate the fruit to create a long rope of peel. Hold the citrus over your cocktail as you cut, so as to catch the oil from the peel.

Cracking Ice If a drink calls for "cracked" ice, take a large ice cube in one hand. Holding a tap-icer in the other, give the ice a smack with the metal end of your tool. This takes some practice, but it should result in two to four smaller pieces.

Crushing Ice This is the kind of ice you'll use for juleps, cobblers, and the like. Take a canvas Lewis bag and fill it with ice. (In a pinch, use a kitchen towel: Place the ice in the middle and fold the corners in, making a mini hobo pack.) Take a wooden ice mallet, or a large wooden muddler, and beat the ice into a consistent sno-cone-like texture. Scoop the ice out of the bag and into proper glassware. Using a Lewis bag, with its water-absorbing canvas material, results in "dry" crushed ice.

Flaming Peel When you have mastered the citrus peel garnish, bring on the pyrotechnics. Cut a citrus peel the same way, but make it shorter and more oval, so it can be more easily handled with one hand. Strike a wooden match (we prefer a match to a lighter, which can impart an unpleasant butane flavor) and let the sulfur burn off. Hold the flame over the cocktail and the peel over the flame until the skin is slightly warmed and the oils have come to the surface, 10 to 15 seconds. Squeeze the peel toward the flame, so the oils flare up as they pass through.

Measuring Gone are the days of eyeballing a pour of your favorite spirit and topping it with Coke or some other syrupy and bubbly mixture. Those drinks are bland and subpar. This book contains recipes with wonderfully expressive, sometimes outrageously bitter, and often funky, ingredients that require your care and attention. We preach the cost savings of measuring your spirits. From a drinker's perspective, it's really about consistency. We do believe that cocktails, like jazz, another great American contribution to culture, can be improvisational. But like all great jazz players, you have to know the standards before you can riff on them. Fill jiggers to the top, and be exacting with smaller measurements.

Muddling Muddling should really be called pressing. It releases the fragrant oils in herbs (such as mint in a julep) or the juice and oils in citrus (limes in a Mojito). If making a drink with herbs, a gentle press will release their fragrant oils. Too much grinding can release bitter notes from the chlorophyll. If your drink calls for fruit, press hard enough to release the juice and extract the oils from the skin. If using both, place herbs under the fruit for extra protection.

Rimming Rimming is an edible garnish technique, done by first dipping the rim of a glass in a liquid—usually a citrus juice or simple syrup—and then dipping it in salt, sugar, or a spice blend. The most familiar example would be the lime-and-salt rim on a Margarita.

Rinsing If a cocktail calls for a "rinse" of something, like absinthe in the classic Sazerac, do this in either of two ways: Place a small amount of the liquid (approximately ⅛ ounce) in the glass and swirl it until the sides are well coated. If you have excess liquid, you can discard it or, if this is your home bar, pour it back in the bottle. Alternatively, buy an atomizer, fill it with the rinsing liquid, and give the cocktail glass a few sprays.

Rolling This is a way of gently mixing by tipping the ingredients, usually with ice, back and forth between the two halves of a shaker. A Bloody Mary benefits from this technique.

Stirring versus Shaking James Bond got it all wrong. Stirred, not shaken, is the standard for spirits-only cocktails. As a loose rule, most drinks will fall into one of two categories: (1) pure booze or (2) booze with modifiers. Modifiers are nonalcoholic ingredients like juices, sugars, syrups, fruits, or herbs. If a drink has modifiers, it should be shaken. Shaking this type of drink emulsifies the liquid into a concoction greater than the sum of its parts. An all-booze drink, on the other hand, like a Manhattan (or 007's Martini), needs only to be chilled, not whipped together so violently. Stirring an all-booze drink should create a cold and clear cocktail with less dilution. A Manhattan drinker prefers the taste of booze, and the aesthetics of a calm, clear sea of brown liquor in your cocktail glass is much more pleasing than a brackish and foamy shaken one.

Stirring After building the drink in your mixing glass, add ice. Half a dozen cubes, about 1¼ inches square, will do the job nicely. Using a bar spoon, stir the drink for at least 30 seconds, in a clockwise motion. Stirring should be fluid and relatively quiet. The only sound should be the clink of ice on the side of the glass. No up-and-down motion is necessary. You are trying to achieve a cold, clear drink with no air bubbles. Practice by placing ice and three ounces of water in your glass. Using your bar spoon, start the bowl of the spoon on the bottom of the glass at the 12 o'clock position, push around to the 6 o'clock position, and then continue in the circular motion back up to 12 o'clock. After practicing, this should feel like rolling the spoon bowl around the bottom of the mixing glass.

Shaking Build your cocktail ingredients in the smaller half of a Boston shaker. Add ice to the larger side, filling it about halfway. Tip the smaller side, pouring the ingredients over the ice. Fit the smaller half inside the larger half and tap your hand on the top to make a seal. Hold the sealed shaker with your hands at the top and bottom, making sure the drink won't spill in case the seal is broken. Holding the shaker horizontally, about shoulder high, "throw" the drink out, away from your body, and then back in. With practice, you will find a rhythm for this back-and-forth motion. To unseal, stand the shaker up, with the larger tin on the bottom. Give the bottom shaker an upward smack with your open hand where the two pieces meet, breaking the seal.

Dry Shake The dry shake is used for making cocktails with egg whites. Egg-white cocktails should be foamy and creamy, almost cappuccino-like in texture. To dry shake, place all ingredients in the smaller half of your shaker. Do not add ice yet. Instead, seal the shaker and shake for about 20 to 30 seconds, until you feel the ingredients start to emulsify, taking on a "ropy" feel. Open the shaker, add ice, and reseal. Shake again for at least 15 seconds to chill the cocktail.

Reverse Dry Shake This is a newer method of shaking egg-white drinks. Place all the cocktail ingredients except the egg white in the shaker. Add ice and shake as you would a regular drink. Open the shaker, leaving the drink in the larger tin. Double-strain the drink into the smaller side of the shaker and discard the ice. Add the egg white to the chilled drink, reseal, and shake again, with no ice. Shake until the drink feels thick and emulsified, about 20 seconds. Pour directly into cocktail glass.

Straining stirred drinks When using a mixing glass, or the glass half of a Boston shaker, a julep strainer is efficient. Insert the julep strainer into the glass with bowl side up, or concave. The strainer should lie on the ice at about a 45-degree angle, with the handle pointing up and out of the glass. Grip the glass near the top and place your index finger over the strainer to hold it in place. Tilt the glass and strain the liquid into the cocktail glass.

Straining shaken drinks If you are using a cobbler shaker with a built-in strainer, simply remove the cap and pour the drink into a glass of your choice. Cobbler shakers strain cocktails more slowly than Boston shakers, but twisting your wrist while pouring the cocktail helps speed things up. If you are using a two-piece Boston shaker, leave the shaken mixture in the larger tin. Place a Hawthorne strainer on top of the large tin, spring side down. Grip the tin near the top and place your index finger over the strainer to hold it in place. Pour cocktail into desired glass.

Double-Straining Most shaken drinks can benefit from an additional strain that removes shards of ice, pulp, or other debris. This can be easily done by placing a conical, fine mesh strainer between the cocktail glass and a Hawthorne-strainer-topped Boston tin. Pour the cocktail through the additional strainer. If the flow is slow, tap the conical strainer with the bottom of the shaker tin to help things along.

Syrups The syrups below appear throughout the recipe section of this book. While some recipes call for the slightly richer flavor of turbinado syrup, simple syrup is generally an acceptable substitute. If you make a lot of cocktails at home, it's worth keeping simple syrup on hand. It's also great in iced tea and iced coffee because there are no pesky crystals to dissolve.

SIMPLE SYRUP

1 cup water

1 cup white granulated sugar

Place sugar and water in a small saucepan, set over high heat, and bring to a boil. Boil for 3 minutes. Remove from heat and cool to room temperature. Refrigerate in an airtight container for up to 1 month.
Yield: Approximately 1¾ cups

TURBINADO SYRUP

2 cups turbinado sugar (light brown cane sugar with large crystals)

1 cup water

Place sugar and water in a small saucepan, set over high heat, and bring a boil. Boil for 3 minutes. Remove from heat and cool to room temperature. Refrigerate in an airtight container for up to 1 month.
Yield: Approximately 2 cups

PINEAPPLE SYRUP

½ pineapple, peeled, cored, and cubed

2 cups water

2 cups white granulated sugar

Place pineapple in a heatproof container and set aside. Place the water and sugar in a medium saucepan, set over high heat, and bring to a boil. Boil for 3 minutes, remove from heat, and pour over pineapple. Cover and refrigerate for 24 hours. Strain through a fine mesh strainer, pressing as much juice as possible out of the pineapple. Refrigerate syrup in airtight container for up to 1 month.
Yield: Approximately 3 cups

GINGER SYRUP

1 cup water

1 cup white granulated sugar

¼ cup peeled and grated ginger

Place sugar and water in a small saucepan, set over high heat, and bring to a boil. Boil for 3 minutes. Add ginger, remove from heat, cover, and steep for 1 hour. Strain out ginger. Refrigerate syrup in an airtight container for up to 1 month.
Yield: Approximately 2 cups

Glassware

As with the tools, you don't need to run out and buy a new set of glasses for your hobby. Consider investing in the glass that corresponds to your signature cocktail. Beyond that, take these as suggestions—and remember there are gems to be found at your local thrift or antique store.

Champagne Flute a slender tulip-shaped stemmed glass used for sparkling wine, and for champagne drinks like a Seelbach Cocktail or many versions of the French 75.

Collins Glass a narrow, straight-sided glass for tall drinks mixed with water or sparkling modifiers like soda water. Also known as a highball glass.

Julep Cup a metal tumbler, often silver, silver plated, or pewter, used for juleps or cobblers. When the drink is built and stirred properly, an icy frosting develops on the outside of the cup. (Silver is a better thermal conductor than pewter, meaning it will get colder faster.)

Rocks Glass a low, wide glass perfect for liquor neat or for a cocktail served "on the rocks." Also known as an old-fashioned glass. Look for a 10- to 12-ounce glass with heft to it. Your whiskey will thank you.

Coupe a stemmed glass with a wide, shallow bowl, also referred to as a champagne coupe or a cocktail glass. While originally intended for champagne, it was co-opted by bartenders as early as the 1930s. The shape and size (easier to handle than a martini glass) is great for any drink served "up," meaning without ice. Holding the glass by the stem prevents the drink from warming too quickly. Most coupes hold 5 to 6 ounces, a snug fit for a well-made cocktail.

Cocktail Glass a stemmed glass with steeper sides than a coupe and a wider bowl than a martini glass. Intended for cocktails served up (with no ice), it usually holds 5 to 6 ounces. If you do not have a cocktail glass, substitute a coupe, and vice versa.

Martini Glass a stemmed glass with sloping sides, an inverted cone. This is an alternative to a coupe or other cocktail glass. Although extra-large versions were popular in the 1980s and 1990s, try to find glasses no larger than 6 to 8 ounces.

Drink Categories

Did you know that "cocktail" actually started out as a specific kind of mixed drink, before it was the catch-all term we use today (see page 97)? Here's a guide to nomenclature.

Collins a sour, often made with lemon juice, and served with ice and soda water

Cobbler similar to a julep, sometimes made with fortified wine instead of a spirit, and with a large seasonal fruit garnish

Crusta a cocktail "crusted" with a sugar rim and garnished with the peel of an entire lemon or orange lining the glass

Daisy a sour that uses a liqueur or grenadine or raspberry syrup as the sweetener ("margarita" is the Spanish word for daisy, and the Margarita is a daisy drink itself)

Fizz a collins with no ice and, usually, the addition of egg white

Flip a base spirit with a whole egg and a sweetener, usually finished with a grating of nutmeg

Frappé a base spirit, sometimes sweetened, served over crushed ice

Highball a base spirit mixed with water or a carbonated beverage and served over ice in a tall glass

Julep a base spirit with mint and sugar, served over crushed ice; also known as a smash

Rickey a collins with lime juice and little or no sweetener

Sour a base spirit with citrus juice and sweetener

Toddy a base spirit, usually sweetened, served hot, and sometimes garnished with citrus or spice

The Future of Southern Drinking

HISTORIOGRAPHY IS A SCIENCE more or less like ballistics: The careful plotting of where a phenomenon has been enables you to predict where it is going. If only the world were thus! But the future, as history shows us, is essentially impervious to investigation. Sure, every once in a while somebody smart or lucky manages to plot a through-line, like when Isaac Asimov predicted the Internet in 1988. But that happens so rarely as to make individual attempts at prediction as reliable as trickle-down economics. Still, it's kinda fun to try.

In, say, fifty years, I predict that Southern drinking will be very different from drinking in the rest of the United (or, by then, Disunited) States. Twenty-first-century drinkers have shown disdain for the centralization and homogenization that dominated twentieth-century tippling. They have embraced the small-scale and the localized. By 2067 that will have given us a South where new-wave agrarianism, rooted in the eighteenth- and nineteenth-century idea of the South as an agricultural paradise where you can grow the best of everything, coupled with the craft movement with all its self-consciously traditionalist ways, will have kicked up a whole range of new-old Southern drinks. There will be local wines, made from cleverly hybridized grape varietals whose DNA is largely American. There will be beer, of course, made in every county that allows it and often flavored with items from the Southern larder. Cowpea-chicory stout, anyone? No doubt Southern soft drinks will extend their recombinant ways in new directions—for all I know, the drink of the South in 2067 will be an electric-blue chili-mango soda sweetened with local cane sugar (I'll get to that) and factory-spiked with legal, synthetic THC.

There will also be a lot of spirits. Historically, the South was a land where the native grapes were nasty and the imported ones were louse food; a land too hot to brew beer. It was all about the spirits, and if there's one thing current trends tell us, it's that hooch is back to stay.

Whiskey, of course, is made everywhere. In half a century, one can hope, it will all be well distilled and fully matured. (One can hope.) But there will also be a whole lot of other stuff. A look at American distilling manuals from the early days of the republic, before whiskey chased off all its competitors, reveals a startling range of crops that were once distilled in the region, all ripe for reviving. Some were terrible: Persimmon brandy was notoriously nasty. Some were indifferent: Cornstalk rum, distilled from the juice contained in the stalks before they put forth ears, was generally thought to be pretty good if it was made well, even if it usually wasn't. Some were good: pawpaw brandy, apple brandy, and whiskeys made from various grains. Even Lowcountry rice produced a decent liquor. One spirit was considered so excellent that it cost more than the finest imported cognac: peach brandy from the Carolinas and Georgia, distilled from fresh peaches and their crushed pits and aged for many years in oak.

Fifty years from now, I have no doubt that somewhere in the South these spirits and drinks will be crafted, sold, and shaken or stirred into cocktails, flips, punches, coolers, and what-have-you. With many of them we're already well on the way.

DW

Acknowledgments

SARA CAMP'S ACKNOWLEDGMENTS

I am grateful to my colleagues at the Southern Foodways Alliance for giving me the opportunity and time to work on this book with all of you. Thanks especially to Melissa, Mary Beth, and John T. for flexing their editorial muscles during my maternity leave. I am so lucky to work with you. Thank you, Jerry, for being an enthusiastic and knowledgeable coeditor and a pleasure to work with, and for responding to copious questions about tasting notes while I was pregnant and out of commission for drink testing. Thank you to all of the bartenders who contributed drink recipes, and to Vishwesh Bhatt for the snack recipes. A massive thanks to Tamie Cook for expert testing. Andy Lee, your photos make this book so pretty, I almost don't mind whether people actually read it. (Actually, I really do hope they read it, but the photos are snazzy, too.) Thanks to Miles Macquarrie and Bryan Rackley of Kimball House for hosting our photo shoot, and to the debonair Thom Driver for lending your styling talents and props. Thank you, Krista Slater, for your myriad contributions, including mixing drinks and serving as a hand model. Shyretha Sheats, thank you for your hand modeling as well. Thank you to Katie King for meticulous fact checking. And a huge thanks to Pat Allen at UGA Press for his enthusiasm in bringing this project to fruition.

Jerry and I consulted many, many books, articles, and websites in researching this guide. We offer a special thanks to the following authors, whose work was an immense help in informing our own: Wayne Curtis (*And a Bottle of Rum*), Robert Moss (*Southern Spirits*), Brad Thomas Parsons (*Bitters* and *Amaro*), and David Wondrich (*Imbibe!* and *Punch*).

Thanks to my wonderful, supportive family and to my husband, Kirk, who is the world's best cheerleader and my favorite drinking buddy. And to our favorite Oxford bartenders past and present at City Grocery and Snackbar, for pouring the Barbary Corsairs, the glasses (okay, bottles) of sauvignon blanc and Sancerre, the gin-and-sodas, the greyhounds, and the scotches: Jayce, Bryan, Alex, Will, Kelly, Ivy, and Cooney.

JERRY'S ACKNOWLEDGMENTS

I thank the Southern Foodways Alliance and all of its members who have taught me, inspired me, and made me feel welcome for the last fifteen years. To my coeditor Sara Camp Arnold Milam—you are a prodigious talent. To John T. Edge, for all you do (including snorts) and for asking me to be a part of this project. To Andrew Thomas Lee and Tamie Cook for making the book look and taste good. To Greg Best, for being a friend, an inspiration, and a cast-iron skillet coconspirator. To Julian Goglia for lifelines and motorcycle trips. To Paul, Shannon, Miles, Kellie, Ben, Mercedes, Tiffanie, and the Atlanta bartending community for setting the cocktail South on fire.

To Charlie Trotter, for the nervous stomachaches and for showing me that manners and excellence are not mutually exclusive but are both worth striving toward. To Larry Hollingsworth, who appreciated my intellect but made sure I knew my numbers, and for being a role model for what it means to be a man in the South. To Ronni Lundy, who taught me to roll up my sleeves and get busy, and to love the place you are from. To Chuck Reece, for letting me play a small part in a special project and for one fine ordination. To Angie Mosier, a friend and a champion of friends. To Todd Richards, for brotherhood and laughter (people need to know how funny you are).

To my parents Kemron and Janet Gayle Johnson, who have always believed in me. And to my wife, Krista Lark Slater, who not only contributed beautiful illustrations to this project but who loves me, inspires me, and makes me a better person.

Credits

GENERAL

Photography—Andrew Thomas Lee

Cocktail photos shot at Kimball House, Decatur, Georgia

Photo Styling—Thom Driver

Props—Thom Driver, Ryan Hancock, Kimball House, Angie Mosier, Krista and Jerry Slater

Food Recipes—Vishwesh Bhatt

Recipe Testing—Tamie Cook

Hand models—Shyretha Sheats, Jerry Slater, Krista Slater

ESSAYS

"I'll Take My Chances," by Kat Kinsman, appearing as the introduction to chapter 3, is adapted from *Gravy* quarterly and reprinted by permission of the author.

"[Pop]Corn from a Jar," by Mark Essig, appearing as a sidebar to chapter 7, is adapted from *Gravy* quarterly and reprinted by permission of the author.

"Keepers of Chipped Dreams," by Gustavo Arellano, appearing as a sidebar to chapter 8, is adapted from *Gravy* quarterly and reprinted by permission of the author.

COCKTAIL RECIPES, IN ORDER OF APPEARANCE

Brandy Milk Punch—Brennan's restaurant

Rum Milk Punch—Erin Ashford

Harry's Bloody Mary—adapted by Jerry Slater from *Harry's ABC of Mixing Cocktails*

Michelada—adapted by Jerry Slater from Joe Ray for *Bon Appétit* magazine

Pimm's Cup—adapted by Jerry Slater from the Napoleon House, New Orleans

Gunshop Fizz—Neal Bodenheimer, Kirk Estopinal, and Maksym Pazniak

Ruby Slipper—Jerry Slater

Paloma—Jerry Slater

Ramos Gin Fizz—adapted by Jerry Slater and Miles Macquarrie from Henry Charles "Carl" Ramos

Kimball House Gin Fizz—Miles Macquarrie

Pendennis Club Cocktail—adapted by Jerry Slater from Ted Haigh, *Vintage Spirits and Forgotten Cocktails*

Seersucker—Jayce McConnell and Drew Stevens

Daisy Buchanan—Jerry Slater

Nihilist Sour—Greg Best

Gris-Gris Sour—Kellie Thorn

Old Spanish—Paul Calvert

General's Orders—Derek Brown

Saved by Zero—Jerry Slater

Risk—Steva Casey

French 75—adapted by Jerry Slater from Jeffrey Morgenthaler, *The Bar Book*

Hannah's French 75—Chris Hannah

Pasture 75—Beth Dixon

Howitzer—Neal Bodenheimer

Seelbach Cocktail—adapted by Jerry Slater from Adam Seger

Fear and Loathing in Louisville—Jerry Slater

Hoisted Petard—Drew Stevens and Alex von Hardberger

Snake-Bit Sprout—Kenneth Freeman and
    Alba Huerta

Cumberland Sour—Matt Tocco

Summer Shandy—Erin Ashford

Mint Julep—Jerry Slater

First Julep—adapted by Jerry Slater from Alba
    Huerta and David Wondrich

Sparkling Julep—Alba Huerta

Oregano Cobbler—Alba Huerta

Ticonderoga Cup—Greg Best and Paul Calvert

Lowcountry Julep—David Wondrich

Absinthe Frappé—Miles Macquarrie

Bourbon Crush—Gary Crunkleton

Bufala Negra—Jerry Slater

Bill Smith's Shortcut Mint Julep—Bill Smith

Hurricane—Chris Hannah

Classic Daiquiri—Jerry Slater

Creole Crusta—Alba Huerta

The Moviegoer—Chris Hannah

Virginia Creeper—Jerry Slater

The Lurleen—Jayce McConnell

Southern Cola—Greg Best

I'm Your Huckleberry—Jerry Slater

Grasshopper—adapted by Jerry Slater from
    Tujague's restaurant, New Orleans

Manhattan—Jerry Slater

The Bellman—Miles Macquarrie

The Socialist—Paul Calvert

The Bitter Southerner #1—Jerry Slater

Kimball House—Miles Macquarrie

The Prestidigitator—Jerry Slater

Fightin' Words—Eric Bennett

Edgewood—Greg Best

McKinney's Pond—Hunt Revell

Old-Fashioned—Jerry Slater

Sherried Old-Fashioned—Derek Brown

Rum Old-Fashioned—Jerry Slater

Añejo Old-Fashioned—Jerry Slater

The Unvanquished—Navarro Carr

Canebrake Cooler—David Wondrich

7th Ward—Matt McFerron

Sazerac—Jerry Slater

Armagnac Sazerac—Alba Huerta

Sazerac Sour—Miles Macquarrie

Li'l Liza Jane—Jerry Slater

Rhythm and Soul—Greg Best

Nite Tripper—Chris Hannah

Pullman Porter—Navarro Carr

Spaghetti Western—Jerry Slater

Vieux Carré—Jerry Slater, adapted from the
    Hotel Monteleone's Carousel Bar

The Old Square—Miles Macquarrie

Two-World Hero—Kellie Thorn

Cab Calloway—Tiffanie Barriere

Negroni—Jerry Slater

Boulevardier—Jerry Slater

Savannah Rosa—Matt McFerron

Bitter Heart—Navarro Carr

The Hardest Walk—Neal Bodenheimer and
    Turk Dietrich

Chatham Artillery Punch—David Wondrich

Buford Highway Artillery Punch—Jerry Slater

AWP 290 Punch—Jerry Slater

Watermelon Sangria—Beth Dixon

Olde Thyme Punch—Jayce McConnell

Twelfth Night Punch—Chris Hannah

Chinese Grocery Five-Treasures Punch—
    David Wondrich

PHOTOS OF CONTRIBUTORS

Mark Essig—Pableaux Johnson

Andrew Thomas Lee—Frank Ockenfels III

Miles Macquarrie—Andrew Thomas Lee for the
    Bitter Southerner

Jayce McConnell—*Tasting Table*

Kellie Thorn—Emily Dorio

David Wondrich—Brandall Atkinson

(All others courtesy of the contributor)

Bibliography

BOOKS

Arthur, Stanley Clisby. *Famous New Orleans Drinks and How to Mix 'Em*. 1937. Gretna, La.: Pelican, 1984.

Bailey, Mark, and Edward Hemingway. *Hemingway and Bailey's Bartending Guide to Great American Writers*. Chapel Hill, N.C.: Algonquin, 2006.

Barr, Andrew. *Drink: A Social History of America*. New York: Carroll and Graf, 1999.

Burns, Eric. *The Spirits of America: A Social History of Alcohol*. Philadelphia: Temple University Press, 2004.

Carson, Gerald. *The Social History of Bourbon: An Unhurried Account of Our Star-Spangled American Drink*. New York: Dodd, Mead, 1963.

Curtis, Wayne. *And a Bottle of Rum: A History of the New World in Ten Cocktails*. New York: Crown, 2006.

Gee, Denise. *Southern Cocktails*. San Francisco: Chronicle Books, 2007.

Grimes, William. *Straight Up or on the Rocks: The Story of the American Cocktail*. New York: North Point Press, 2001.

Haigh, Ted. *Vintage Spirits and Forgotten Cocktails*. Beverly, Mass.: Quarry Books, 2009.

Hollinger, Jeff, and Rob Schwartz. *The Art of the Bar*. San Francisco: Chronicle Books, 2006.

Kaplan, David, Nick Fauchald, and Alex Day. *Death & Co: Modern Classic Cocktails*. Berkeley, Calif.: Ten Speed Press, 2014.

Kelman, Ari. *A River and Its City: The Nature of Landscape in New Orleans*. Berkeley: University of California Press, 2003.

Kendall, John Smith. *History of New Orleans*. Chicago: Lewis, 1922.

Lender, Mark Edward, and James Kirby Martin. *Drinking in America: A History*. New York: Free Press, 1982.

MacElhone, Harry. *Harry's ABC of Mixing Cocktails*. Paris: Lecram, 1927. Reprinted as *Barflies and Cocktails* (New York: Mud Puddle Books, 2008).

Mintz, Sidney W. *Sweetness and Power: The Place of Sugar in Modern History*. New York: Viking, 1985.

Morgenthaler, Jeffrey. *The Bar Book: Elements of Cocktail Technique*. With Martha Holmberg. San Francisco: Chronicle Books, 2014.

Moss, Robert F. *Southern Spirits: Four Hundred Years of Drinking in the American South, with Recipes*. Berkeley, Calif.: Ten Speed Press, 2016.

Parsons, Brad Thomas. *Amaro: The Spirited World of Bittersweet, Herbal Liqueurs, with Cocktails, Recipes, and Formulas*. Berkeley, Calif.: Ten Speed Press, 2016.

———. *Bitters: A Spirited History of a Classic Cure-All, with Cocktails, Recipes, and Formulas*. Berkeley, Calif.: Ten Speed Press, 2011.

Pulos, Arthur J. *The American Design Adventure, 1940–1975*. Cambridge, Mass.: MIT Press, 1988.

Roahen, Sara. *Gumbo Tales: Finding My Place at the New Orleans Table*. New York: W. W. Norton, 2009.

Rorabaugh, W. J. *The Alcoholic Republic: An American Tradition*. New York: Oxford University Press, 1979.

Weaver, H. Dwight. *Missouri Caves in History and Legend*. Columbia: University of Missouri Press, 2008.

Williams, Elizabeth M., and Chris McMillian. *Lift Your Spirits: A Celebratory History of Cocktail Culture in New Orleans*. Baton Rouge: Louisiana State University Press, 2016.

Williams, Tennessee. *Cat on a Hot Tin Roof*. New York: New Directions, 1955.

Wondrich, David. *Imbibe! From Absinthe Cocktail to Whiskey Smash, a Salute in Stories and Drinks to "Professor" Jerry Thomas, Pioneer of the American Bar*. Rev. ed. New York: Tarcher Perigee, 2015.

———. *Punch: The Delights (and Dangers) of the Flowing Bowl*. New York: Tarcher Perigee, 2010.

ARTICLES

Asimov, Eric. "In the Big Easy, Two Cocktails Reign." *New York Times*, July 16, 2008.

Baiocchi, Talia. "Want to Make Better Cocktails? Crush Your Own Ice." *Bon Appétit*, April 2015.

Balestier, Courtney. "Let Us Now Retire the Whiskey Woman." *Punch*, November 17, 2015.

Biography.com. "Marquis de Lafayette." biography.com/people/marquis-de-lafayette-21271783.

Bonesteel, Matt. "How to Make a Kentucky Derby–Worthy Mint Julep." *Washington Post*, May 5, 2016.

Branley, Edward. "NOLA History: Apothecaries, Drug Stores and Pharmacy in New Orleans." GoNola.com, July 29, 2013. gonola.com/tag/new-orleans-pharmacy.

Causey, Donna R. "Actress Lillian Russell Discovered the Anguish of Chigger Bites in Alabama." *Alabama Pioneers*, February 27, 2016.

Cecchini, Toby. "The Secret Signature Cocktail of Louisville." *Saveur*, October 2015.

Coleman, Dash. "Savannah's Pinkie Master's: The Rest of the Story." *Savannah Morning News*, January 9, 2016.

Conte, Robert. "The Story of the Mint Julep." *Greenbrier Culinary Community*, November 20, 2009.

Curtis, Wayne. "Reconsidering Armagnac, the Rebel of Brandy." *Punch*, February 9, 2015.

DeJesus, Erin. "It's Not Easy Being Green: The Weird History of the Grasshopper." *Eater*, October 23, 2014.

Emen, Jake. "An Exhaustive Guide to Fortified Wines." *Eater*, April 12, 2016.

Farrell, Shanna. "What Does It Mean to Drink like a Woman?" *Punch*, March 31, 2014.

Hesser, Amanda. "Recipe Redux, 1935: Ramos Gin Fizz." *New York Times*, June 15, 2008.

Houston, Rick. "NASCAR's Earliest Days Forever Connected to Bootlegging." NASCAR.com, November 1, 2012. nascar.com/en_us/news-media/articles/2012/11/01/moonshine-mystique.html.

Kazek, Kelly. "Bangor Cave Was Once Popular Underground Speakeasy, Casino." AL.com, October 5, 2014. al.com/living/index.ssf/2014/10/bangor_cave_was_once_popular_u.html.

———. "On Repeal Day: 7 Places Alabamians Bought Illicit Liquor During Prohibition, Including Speakeasy Caves, Underground Tunnels." AL.com, December 5, 2014. al.com/living/index.ssf/2014/12/on_repeal_day_7_places_alabami.html.

Lopez, Ashley. "Meet the First Woman Master Bourbon Distiller in Modern Times." WFPL (Louisville), November 16, 2015. wfpl.org/meet-the-first-woman-master-bourbon-distiller-in-modern-times/.

Lynch, David. "How to Drink Vermouth, Beyond the Martini." *Bon Appétit*, March 2015.

Mariani, John. "The Secret Origins of the Bloody Mary." *Esquire*, February 2014.

McKeithan, Seán. "Every Ounce a Man's Whiskey? Bourbon in the White Masculine South." *Southern Cultures* 18, no. 1 (Spring 2012).

Miles, Jonathan. "Mint Julep: A Drink for All Seasons." *Garden & Gun*, May/June 2008.

Morse, Minna Scherlinder. "Chilly Reception." *Smithsonian*, July 2002.

Nims, Brittany C. "Restoring Wonderland." *Arkansas Traveler*, April 11, 2014.

Orchant, Rebecca. "Swedish Punsch: Kronan Brings It Back from the Brink." *Huffington Post*, January 14, 2013. huffingtonpost.com/2013/01/14/swedish-punsch-kronan_n_2458913.html.

Ossman, David. "Cab Calloway." *Jazz Profiles*, National Public Radio, n.d. npr.org/programs/jazzprofiles/archive/calloway.html.

Percy, Walker. "Bourbon, Neat." *Claremont Review of Books*, November 28, 2001. claremont.org/crb/article/bourbon-neat/. Excerpted from "Bourbon" in *Signposts in a Strange Land*, ed. Patrick Samway (New York: Farrar, Straus and Giroux, 1991).

Punch. "Bringing It Back Bar: What to Do with Bénédictine." November 2, 2015.

——— . "Bringing It Back Bar: What to Do with Strega." April 27, 2015.

Ray, Joe. "How They Make Micheladas in Mexico." *Bon Appétit*, May 2013.

Regan, Gaz. "A Cocktail Good Enough for Gatsby to Love." *SFGate*, July 28, 2005.

Rodbard, Matt. "Meet Kentucky's First Female Master Distiller Since Prohibition." *Saveur*, March 2016.

Shoffner, Robert. "Here's to the Bloody Mary." *Washingtonian*, July 2008.

Simonson, Robert. "That Historic Cocktail? Turns Out It's a Fake." *New York Times*, October 31, 2016.

Tucker, Greg. "Caves Concealed Runaways, Rebels, and Revelers." Rutherford County (Tennessee) Historical Society, February 24, 2013.

Wondrich, David. "The Cunningest Compounders of Beverages: The Hidden History of African Americans Behind the Bar." *Bitter Southerner*, January 12, 2016.

MULTIMEDIA

Curtis, Wayne. "Walking the Neutral Ground." Presented at SFA Summer Symposium, 2015. Audio. soundcloud.com/southernfoodwaysalliance/wayne-curtis-walking-the-neutral-ground.

Department of Alcoholic Beverage Control, Commonwealth of Kentucky. "Kentucky's Wet and Dry Counties." Map. 2012.

Grisham, John. "John Grisham Reads Soggy Sweat's Whiskey Speech." Presented at Oxford Conference for the Book, 2010. Video, Southern Documentary Project. youtube.com/watch?v=qPzUcJcgXUA.

Rutherford County (Tennessee) Historical Society. "Black Cat Cave." News video, September 18, 2015. youtube.com/watch?v=_anKNLyr_D8.

Southern Foodways Alliance. Bartender oral histories. Audio interviews, New Orleans 2005 by Amy C. Evans, New Orleans 2015 by Rien Fertel with photographs by Denny Culbert, Louisville 2007 by Amy C. Evans. Under southernfoodways.org/oral-history.

York, Joe. *Marsaw.* Documentary film on Martin Sawyer, made for SFA, 2006. southernfoodways.org/a-fresh-look-marsaw/.

Contributors

Gustavo Arellano Arellano is the editor of *OC Weekly*, an alternative newspaper in Orange County, California, and the author of *Taco USA: How Mexican Food Conquered America*. He writes *¡Ask a Mexican!*, a nationally syndicated column with a circulation of 2 million in nearly 40 newspapers across the United States. He is a columnist for the Southern Foodways Alliance's *Gravy* quarterly.

Erin Ashford Ashford, a native of Florida, has made Austin, Texas, her home since 2008. An alumna of the bar programs at Blackbird & Henry and Qui, she is now the bar manager at Olamaie. She creates drink menus for both dinner and brunch, supplementing classic cocktails with her own creations.

Tiffanie Barriere Barriere mixed drinks at One Flew South in Atlanta's Hartsfield-Jackson International Airport from 2008 to 2016, keeping thirsty travelers happy. She is an active member of Atlanta's dynamic cocktail scene and is often known by her nickname "The Drinking Coach," due to her passion for and knowledge of spirits and their history. She is a past secretary of the Atlanta chapter of the United States Bartenders' Guild, a member of the Southern Foodways Alliance, and a frequent speaker and guest bartender at cocktail challenge events and festivals around the Southeast. She is currently working with chef Duane Nutter, her former colleague at One Flew South, on a new restaurant, Southern National, in Mobile, Alabama.

Eric Bennett Bennett, a native of Birmingham, Alabama, has been bartending since his days as a college student at Birmingham-Southern. Most recently he managed the bar program at Carrigan's Public House. He loves to travel, study food and beverage history, and attend cocktail competitions and culinary festivals to brush up on his craft.

Greg Best
A native of Poughkeepsie, New York, Greg Best is now a proud Atlantan. During his tenure as a founding partner and head barkeep at Holeman and Finch Public House, the restaurant was a James Beard nominee for Outstanding Bar Program. He has contributed recipes to numerous cocktail books, magazines, and websites and is a contributing writer for the *Local Palate*. In a TEDx Atlanta talk, Best described his vocation as "social chemist." He is now a proprietor of Ticonderoga Club in Inman Park, where the "Yankee heritage" (his term) of the tavern's cofounders informs the atmosphere and offerings in their Atlanta home.

Vishwesh Bhatt is the chef at Snackbar in Oxford, Mississippi. A native of Ahmedabad in the Indian state of Gujarat, he moved to the United States to attend college at the University of Kentucky. He is a three-time James Beard Award finalist for Best Chef: South.

Neal Bodenheimer
Bodenheimer, a native of New Orleans, took his first job behind the bar at age eighteen. Following college at the University of Texas, a yearlong trip around the world, and six years in New York, Bodenheimer returned to New Orleans and opened Cure in 2009. In addition to Cure, which was a 2016 James Beard nominee for Outstanding Bar Program, Bodenheimer also owns and operates the rum-centric bar Cane & Table in the French Quarter and the restaurant Café Henri in the Bywater.

Derek Brown   Brown is the president of Drink Company and the proprietor of four craft cocktail bars in Washington, D.C.: Mockingbird Hill, Eat the Rich, Southern Efficiency, and the Columbia Room, a two-time James Beard award nominee. *Imbibe* magazine named him Bartender of the Year in 2015. Brown is on the boards of the Tequila Interchange Project and the D.C. Public Library Foundation. He is the chief spirits advisor to the National Archives.

Paul Calvert
Calvert has worked in restaurants and bars since he was fifteen. A graduate of the College of Charleston and Georgia State University with degrees in English Literature from both, he currently lives in Atlanta. He has had the honor of working behind some great Atlanta bars, such as the Sound Table and Paper Plane. He is co-owner, along with a few of his closest friends, of Ticonderoga Club, a neighborhood tavern.

Navarro Carr   Carr has spent years developing his knowledge of spirits and mixology, and has taken an integral part in the development of the craft cocktail culture in Atlanta. He also consults within the beverage industry on education, training, event planning, and brand development and is currently the beverage director at the Sound Table, an Atlanta bar, restaurant, and DJ venue.

Steva Casey Casey is the bar manager at Saturn, a live-music venue in Birmingham, Alabama. She has nearly twenty years of experience in the Birmingham service industry, and her recipes and cocktail advice have been published in *Cosmopolitan*, *CNN*, and *Men's Journal*. She believes that the most important part of her job as a bartender is to be a good host. Known as the unofficial "Ambassador of Birmingham," Casey often travels to expand her palate and to spread the gospel of Birmingham food and drink culture.

Gary Crunkleton Crunkleton has been bartending in Chapel Hill, North Carolina, for a quarter century, beginning as an undergraduate at UNC Chapel Hill. He is the owner of the Crunkleton, a craft cocktail bar in Chapel Hill. When he is not behind the bar, Crunkleton takes off his signature bow tie to spend time with his wife, Megan, and their three sons.

Beth Dixon Dixon grew up on a historic farm in Beaverdam, Virginia. She has worked in restaurants in Richmond for fifteen years, tending bar for twelve. In addition to mixing drinks, Dixon loves canning and preserving and is an amateur beekeeper.

John T. Edge Edge is the founding director of the Southern Foodways Alliance.

Mark Essig Essig is the author of *Lesser Beasts: A Snout-to-Tail History of the Humble Pig* and *Edison & the Electric Chair*. He has written for *Gravy*, the *New York Times*, and the *Los Angeles Times*, among other publications. He holds a Ph.D. in U.S. history from Cornell University. A native of St. Louis, he lives in Asheville, North Carolina.

Chris Hannah   Hannah has worked in the service industry for twenty-five years, twenty of them behind a bar. For more than a dozen years he has tended bar at Arnaud's French 75 Bar in New Orleans's French Quarter. Under Hannah's direction as bar manager, the French 75 Bar was a 2016 James Beard nominee for Outstanding Bar Program.

Alba Huerta   Huerta is the proprietor of Julep bar in Houston, where she has lived for most of her life. Previously she was general manager of Anvil Bar and Refuge and an opening partner in the Pastry War, also in Houston. Julep was one of *Bon Appétit*'s five best new bars in the nation in 2015, and Huerta was *Imbibe* magazine's 2014 Bartender of the Year and one of *Food & Wine*'s ten rising-star female mixologists in 2015. She serves on the board of directors of the Southern Foodways Alliance.

Kat Kinsman   Kinsman is the senior food and drinks editor for *Extra Crispy*, Time Inc.'s breakfast-centric website. She was the editor-in-chief of *Tasting Table* and the founding editor of CNN's *Eatocracy*. She is also the author of *Hi, Anxiety: Life with a Bad Case of Nerves*.

Andrew Thomas Lee   Lee specializes in food and drink photography and portraits, especially of musicians. His work has been published in *Esquire*, *Bon Appétit*, *Food & Wine*, *Gravy*, and *Garden & Gun*. He lives in Atlanta.

Miles Macquarrie   Macquarrie is the bar director and managing partner of Kimball House in Decatur, Georgia, a three-time James Beard semifinalist for Outstanding Bar Program and named one of the Five Best New Cocktail Bars in the country by *Bon Appétit*. He enjoys using seasonal produce and making his own bitters and tinctures to enhance the flavor of his drinks. Macquarrie has been voted best mixologist multiple times in *Creative Loafing*'s Best of Atlanta. He recently developed his signature Amaro Macquarrie in partnership with BroVo Spirits, a distillery in Washington State.

Jayce McConnell   McConnell began his restaurant career shucking oysters at Snackbar in Oxford, Mississippi.

He soon developed an interest in cocktails and advanced into the role of head bartender, helping Snackbar develop its reputation for craft cocktails that run the gamut from classic to innovative. In 2013 he moved to Charleston, South Carolina, to direct the bar at Edmund's Oast. He was a 2013 *Eater* Young Gun and one of Zagat's "30 Under 30" food and beverage professionals in Charleston. In addition to his work at Edmund's Oast, McConnell also consults with restaurants beyond Charleston to develop cocktail menus.

Matt McFerron   A native of Arkansas, McFerron opened the Old Pal in Athens, Georgia, with co-owner Daniel Ray in 2013. *Southern Living* magazine named the Old Pal one of the South's Best Bars of 2016. McFerron also produces Buster's Bitters, a line of cocktail bitters named after his dog.

Hunt Revell   Revell is the bar captain at Seabear Oyster Bar in Athens, Georgia. He learned to appreciate a good cocktail at an early age thanks to his grandparents, who loved their "toddy time." In addition to his work behind the bar, he is a contributor to the online magazine *Seed & Plate* and the coach of Athens's Supertonics Co-Ed Level C softball team.

Drew Stevens   A native of Natchez, Mississippi, Stevens has worked with City Grocery Restaurant Group in Oxford since 2003. He is the general manager of Snackbar, which he describes as "an oasis of cocktails, conversation, with the best duck sandwich around." His wife, Jill, manages Big Bad Breakfast next door. Since Snackbar opened in 2010, Stevens has collaborated with Snackbar's bartenders—including Jayce

McConnell, Alex von Hardberger, and Ivy McLellan—to create and name new additions to the cocktail menus.

Kellie Thorn   Thorn, a Georgia native, has been bartending for more than a dozen years. In 2010 she joined the opening team of Hugh Acheson's Empire State South and became beverage director for all of Acheson's restaurants in 2013. She is a Certified Cognac Educator and has passed the BarSmarts Advanced Program and the BAR Five-Day Certification Program. She also helps organize fundraising events for Wholesome Wave Georgia and Community Farmers Markets of Atlanta.

Matt Tocco

Tocco first learned to bartend from Toby Maloney, as one of the opening bartenders of the Patterson House in Nashville, in the spring of 2009. After a three-year tenure at the Patterson House, Tocco became the opening bar manager of Rolf and Daughters. There he garnered national press and developed a devoted local customer base. He went on to conceptualize and open the bar programs at Pinewood Social, Le Sel, and Bastion. While you can still find him behind the bar at the Patterson House from time to time, he spends most days collaboratively developing cocktail menus with his bartenders, managing staff, building educational materials, and mentoring aspiring bartenders.

David Wondrich

Wondrich is the James Beard Award–winning author of *Imbibe!* and *Punch*. He is the longtime drinks correspondent for *Esquire* magazine, the senior drinks correspondent for the *Daily Beast*, and a leading expert on cocktail and spirits history. When he's not writing, Wondrich lectures, develops recipes, consults with bars, educates bartenders, and works with distillers to develop new spirits based on historic techniques.

About the Southern Foodways Alliance

The Southern Foodways Alliance, founded in 1999, documents, studies, and explores the diverse food cultures of the changing American South.

Our work sets a welcome table where all may consider our history and our future in a spirit of respect and reconciliation.

A member-supported organization based at the University of Mississippi's Center for the Study of Southern Culture, we collect oral histories, produce films, sponsor scholarship, mentor students, stage events, and publish *Gravy,* a journal of great writing and a biweekly podcast.

The SFA showcases a South that is constantly evolving. Our work complicates stereotypes, documents new dynamics, and gives voice to the often unsung folk who grow, cook, and serve our daily meals.

Join. Listen. Subscribe. southernfoodways.org

Index of Names

Index of Drinks and Ingredients